James W. Bastien

and

Jane Smisor Bastien

# Beginning Piano for Adults

for

**Any Class of Adult Beginners**
**The Private Student**
**The Classroom Teacher and Education Major**
**The Music Major and Piano Minor**
**Beginning Music Theory**
**Electronic Piano Laboratories**
**The Music Therapy Major**

**General Words & Music Co.**

Ed. No. GP23

*To Lisa and Lori*

# BASTIEN

## SUPPLEMENTARY BOOKS

### CHRISTMAS BOOKS
| | |
|---|---|
| GP42 | Christmas Carols for Two Pianos |
| GP311 | Christmas Duets, Level 1 |
| GP312 | Christmas Duets, Level 2 |
| GP313 | Christmas Duets, Level 3 |
| WP48 | Christmas Favorites, Primer |
| WP49 | Christmas Favorites, Level 1 |
| WP50 | Christmas Favorites, Level 2 |
| WP68 | Christmas Favorites, Level 3 |
| WP69 | Christmas Favorites, Level 4 |
| GPO | Merry Christmas, Vol. 1 |
| GP17 | Merry Christmas, Vol. 2 |
| GP41 | Merry Christmas, Vol 3 |
| WP67 | Nutcracker Suite, The |

### COUNTRY & WESTERN
| | |
|---|---|
| GP66 | Country, Western 'N Folk, Book 1 |
| GP67 | Country, Western 'N Folk, Book 2 |

### DUETS
| | |
|---|---|
| WP60 | Duet Favorites, Level 1 |
| WP61 | Duet Favorites, Level 2 |
| WK2 | Duet Favorites, Level 3 |
| WP63 | Duet Favorites, Level 4 |
| GP22 | Duets for Fun, Book 1 |
| GP43 | Duets for Fun, Book 2 |

### HYMNS
| | |
|---|---|
| GP24 | Hymns for Piano, Book 1 |
| GP25 | Hymns for Piano, Book 2 |
| WP43 | Hymns Favorites, Primer |
| WP44 | Hymns Favorites, Level 1 |
| WP45 | Hymns Favorites, Level 2 |

### PIANO LITERATURE
| | |
|---|---|
| WP42 | Easy Piano Classics |
| WP128 | First Bach Album |
| WP70 | First Piano Repertoire Album |
| GP9 | Piano Literature, Vol. 1 |
| GP10 | Piano Literature, Vol. 2 |
| GP20 | Piano Literature for the Intermediate Grades, Vol. 3 |
| GP57 | Piano Literature for the Early Advanced Grades, Vol. 4 |

### POP & ROCK
| | |
|---|---|
| WP135 | First Pops For Piano |
| WP51 | Pop Piano Styles, Level 1 |
| WP52 | Pop Piano Styles, Level 2 |
| WP53 | Pop Piano Styles, Level 3 |
| WP54 | Pop Piano Styles, Level 4 |
| GP37 | Pop, Rock 'N Blues, Book 1 |
| GP38 | Pop, Rock 'N Blues, Book 2 |
| GP39 | Pop, Rock 'N Blues, Book 3 |

### POPULAR COLLECTIONS
| | |
|---|---|
| WP134 | Bastiens' Best of Bacharach & David |
| WP140 | First Songs Of My Country |
| WP21 | Patriotic Songs for Piano |
| GP90 | Scott Joplin Favorites |
| WP27 | Stephen Foster Favorites |
| GP28 | Walt Disney Favorites |

### PRE-LITERATURE BOOKS
| | |
|---|---|
| GP18 | Playtime at the Piano, Book 1 |
| GPl9 | Playtime at the Piano, Book 2 |

### SOLO COLLECTIONS
| | |
|---|---|
| WP40 | Classic Themes by the Masters |
| WP37 | Favorite Melodies the World Over, Level 1 |
| WP38 | Favorite Melodies the World Over, Level 2 |
| WP41 | Religious Favorites |
| WP83 | Solo Repertoire |

### SONATINA COLLECTIONS
| | |
|---|---|
| WP124 | First Sonatina Album |
| GP302 | First Sonatinas |
| WP408 | More Mini Sonatinas |
| GP97 | Sonatina Favorites, Book 1 |
| GP98 | Sonatina Favorites, Book 2 |
| GP99 | Sonatina Favorites, Book 3 |
| GP310 | Sonatinas for the Seasons |
| WP139 | Three Mini Sonatinas |

## SPECIAL BOOKS

### PARENT'S GUIDE
| | |
|---|---|
| WP29 | A Parent's Guide to Piano Lessons |

### PEDAGOGY TEXT
| | |
|---|---|
| GP40 | How To Teach Piano Successfully |

### TRANSFER STUDENT
| | |
|---|---|
| GP29 | Multi-Key Reading |

## SOLOS

| | |
|---|---|
| WP1050 | Arabesque and Ballade — Burgmüller/Bastien |
| GP186 | Beethoven's 5th |
| GP190 | Bourree—Bach/Bastien |
| GP191 | Concerto in A minor — Vivaldi/Bastien |
| GP177 | Entertainer, The—Joplin/Bastien |
| WP1052 | Für Elise — Beethoven/Bastien |

| | |
|---|---|
| GP188 | Jesu, Joy of Man's Desiring — Bach/Bastien |
| GP182 | Maple Leaf Rag—Joplin/Bastien |
| WP1013 | Marche Militaire — Schubert/Bastien |
| WP1053 | Solfeggietto — C. P. E. Bach/Bastien |
| WP1054 | Sonata in C — Mozart/Bastien |
| WP1055 | Sonatina in C — Clementi/Bastien |
| GP183 | Sonatina in Classic Style |

| | |
|---|---|
| GP185 | Sonatina in Contemporary Style |
| GP184 | Sonatina in Romantic Style |
| WP1056 | Spinning Song — Elmenreich/Bastien |
| GP178 | Toccata |
| GP189 | Toccata in D minor—Bach/Bastien |
| GP187 | Variation on a Theme By Paganini — Paganini/Bastien |

Neil A. Kjos Music Company • Publisher  4380 Jutland Drive • San Diego. CA 92117

# PREFACE

This book is an outgrowth of the authors' extensive experience teaching beginners of all ages in both private and group instruction. The text is designed primarily for students at the college level, either music major or non-music major. It may also be used for any adult or teen-age beginner.

*Beginning Piano for Adults* consists of four sections, each containing carefully selected material to insure gradual, thorough, continuous progress. Special emphasis is given to establishing good reading habits and rhythmic orientation, providing ensemble material, building a thorough technical foundation, and introducing the student to the fundamentals of theory and musical structure.

*Section I, Pre-reading*, is designed for keyboard orientation. *Section II, Reading*, contains graded reading material and a variety of exercises necessary for pianistic development. Various accompaniments are used as harmonizations to folk songs. *Section III, Functional Piano*, is especially important for the music education major, or for students majoring in elementary education. These students must be able to harmonize given melodies with appropriate accompaniments. The melodies are arranged in order, from easy to more difficult. *Section IV, Piano Literature, Technique and Style*, is a continuation of the first two sections and provides ample pianistic reading repertory and related technical and stylistic exercises.

Each aspect of theory cannot be explained in detailed analysis in the body of the text. Therefore the student should be encouraged to study the theory outline given in the back of the book, Appendix A, pp.198-203, and to relate and coordinate his keyboard activity with the explanation found on these pages.

There is sufficient material for four semester's work within this text. It is recommended that Unit 15 not be given until the third semester, as most theory classes do not introduce modulation until the sophomore year. Section IV may be introduced in the first year with the instructor's discretion. Likewise, Section III, Unit 14, may be assigned earlier than it appears in the book.

An expression of thanks is extended to Dr. Patrick McCarty, Assistant Professor of Theory, and to Mr. Charles Braswell, Associate Professor of Music Therapy, both of Loyola University, New Orleans, for reading and suggesting improvements in various portions of the manuscript.

James W. Bastien
and
Jane Smisor Bastien

# CONTENTS

## SECTION TWO
### Reading

# SECTION ONE

## PRE-READING

VENETIAN SPINETTINO (16th Century)
Photo courtesy of the Metropolitan Museum of Art, Pulitzer
Bequest Fund 1953. This instrument was made for Eleanora
d'Este, Duchess of Urbino, 1540. Inscribed on the front strip
above the keys: I am rich in gold and rich in sound; do not
touch me if you have nothing good to play.

# SECTION ONE

## PRE-READING

The first six units (pp. 1-27) are designed to introduce the beginning student to basic, preparatory keyboard skills. The pre-reading melodies with simple rhythm and harmony allow the student to "read" and to "make music" in all keys from the very beginning.

The pre-reading skills established in SECTION ONE include:
1. Developing instinctively good hand position and finger co-ordination.
2. Learning the position-related groups of keys.
3. Learning to play with eyes on the music (playing without visual reference to the keyboard).
4. Counting aloud (providing a good rhythmic orientation).
5. Learning the concept and relationship of skips and steps (intervals) on the keyboard and playing within the basic five-finger position in all keys.
6. Learning to play the I and V7 chords by "feel" only in all keys.
7. Simple transposition according to the concept of the position-related groups of keys.

The combination of physical co-ordination and intellectual understanding which the student develops during the pre-reading period leads logically and naturally to the next step in the learning process, *reading music* or sight-reading (SECTION TWO).

# UNIT 1

- Direction on the keyboard
- How the fingers are numbered
- The five finger position
- The tonic chord

## DIRECTION ON THE KEYBOARD

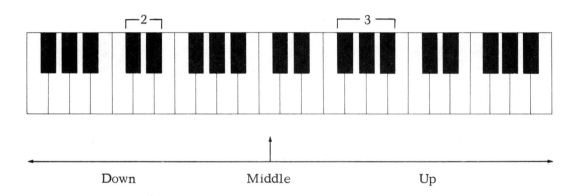

Down       Middle       Up

Sit directly in the middle of the keyboard. Play some HIGH (white) keys with your Right Hand and some LOW (white) keys with your Left Hand.

Notice the grouping of black keys into two's and three's. Play some HIGH black key groups and some LOW black key groups.

The MELODY or PITCH will go higher as your fingers move to the RIGHT and LOWER as your fingers move to the LEFT.

## MELODIC DIRECTION

A melody is constructed of varying pitches. Some tones go up, some tones go down, and some are repeated.

Sing *Merrily We Roll Along* and shape the melody in the air with your hands to establish a "feel" for melodic contour.

Right Hand

  a - long;

Mer - ri - ly we roll a - long, roll a - long, roll

Left Hand

Mer - ri - ly we roll a - long, o'er the deep blue sea.

# Unit I
## HOW THE FINGERS ARE NUMBERED

Left Hand                     Right Hand

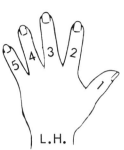      

Since correct fingering is necessary for fluent and facile playing, practice saying these finger numbers aloud, moving the corresponding fingers up and down. Learn these finger numbers so they become automatic.

As finger numbers are called out by the instructor, play the correct fingers in the air.

### 1. MERRILY WE ROLL ALONG

---

**DIRECTED SELF-STUDY**
1. Sing the words and clap the rhythm to this song.
2. "Play" the song in the air singing the finger numbers aloud.
3. Find the position for both hands.
4. Keep eyes on the book following the numbers at the bottom of the page.
5. Play through first with the Right Hand (R.H.) then with the Left Hand (L.H.), singing the finger numbers aloud.

---

## POSITION for MERRILY WE ROLL ALONG

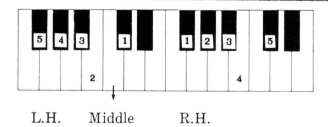

L.H.      Middle      R.H.

Right Hand

3  2  1  2  3  3  3      2  2  2      3  5  5      3  2  1  2  3  3  3      2  2  3  2  1

Mer-ri-ly we roll a-long,  roll a-long,  roll a-long;  Mer-ri-ly we roll a-long,  o'er the deep blue sea.

Left Hand

3  4  5  4  3  3  3      4  4  4      3  1  1      3  4  5  4  3  3  3      4  4  3  4  5

# Unit 1
## THE FIVE FINGER POSITION

A FIVE FINGER POSITION (sometimes referred to as a five finger scale, or penta-scale) uses the first five tones of a (Major) scale. (There are twelve Major scales, and each one is made up of eight tones.) *

Learn to play the three suggested positions given here. You may also play five finger positions starting on other keys on the keyboard using your "ear" as a guide. Add the necessary black and white keys to form the correct sounding five tones within these other positions.

Play LEGATO. Connect one finger to another so the tones are as smooth sounding as possible.

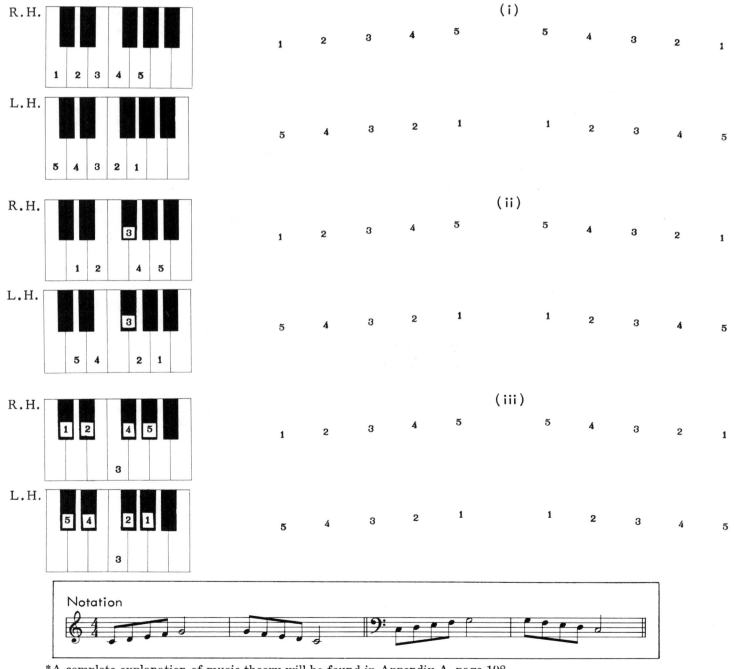

> DIRECTED SELF-STUDY
> 1. "Play" the five finger position in the air singing the finger numbers aloud.
> 2. Find the position for both hands.
> 3. Keep eyes on the book.
> 4. Play through first with the Right Hand then with the Left Hand, singing the finger numbers aloud.

*A complete explanation of music theory will be found in Appendix A, page 198.

# Unit I

## THE TONIC CHORD (I Chord)

A CHORD is the simultaneous sounding of several tones, usually three or more. The I chord (or tonic chord) is formed from three of the notes used in a five finger position. When these three notes are played at the same time they form a chord (or triad). Chords provide the HARMONY used in accompaniments.

To form a chord, begin with a five finger position, then:

$$\text{The Right Hand plays} \quad \begin{cases} 5 \\ 3 \\ 1 \end{cases} \text{at the same time.}$$

$$\text{The Left Hand plays} \quad \begin{cases} 1 \\ 3 \\ 5 \end{cases} \text{at the same time.}$$

Play the tonic chords for the suggested positions below, first with the Left Hand (L.H.), then with the Right Hand (R.H.), and finally, play both hands together at the same time.

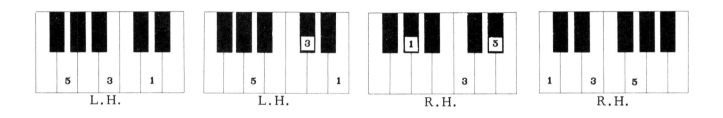

2. THE FARMER IN THE DELL

Sing the words and play I chords to *The Farmer in the Dell* at the same time. Use the above positions or any that you choose.

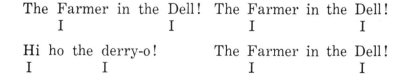

# UNIT 2

- The piano keyboard and the musical alphabet
- Rhythmic notation (4/4 time)
- The group I keys
- The arpeggio

## THE PIANO KEYBOARD AND THE MUSICAL ALPHABET

The Musical Alphabet names the white keys on the keyboard.
The same seven letters (A,B,C,D,E,F,G) are used over and over.

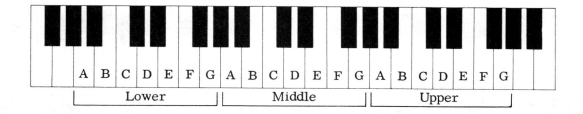

Practice playing the Musical Alphabet BOTH forward and backward on the keyboard in different registers (low, middle, high). Use the second finger (either hand) for playing the seven tones, and say the alphabet letter names aloud while playing.

Learn the individual names of the white keys in relation to the black key groups. The white key between the two black key group is D. Play all the D's on the piano. The white key to the right of the three black key group is B. Play all the B's on the piano, etc. Find various white keys dictated by the instructor.

## SHARPS AND FLATS

A SHARP (♯) raises the pitch of a note a half step to the closest key above.
A FLAT (♭) lowers the pitch of a note a half step to the closest key below.
A HALF STEP is the closest distance on the piano. From any key to the next one (black or white) is a half step.

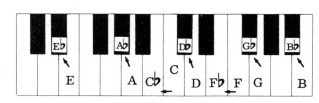

Play these keys as SHARPS:  C,G,F,A,D,E,B
Play these keys as FLATS:    D,E,A,G,B,C,F

# Unit 2
## RHYTHMIC NOTATION

NOTES indicate two things: PITCH (the highness or lowness of sound)
DURATION (the number of counts to be held)

Below are several frequently used kinds of notes found in 4/4, 3/4, or 2/4 time. CLAP AND COUNT THEIR VALUES ALOUD.

KIND OF NOTE                                    METHOD OF COUNTING

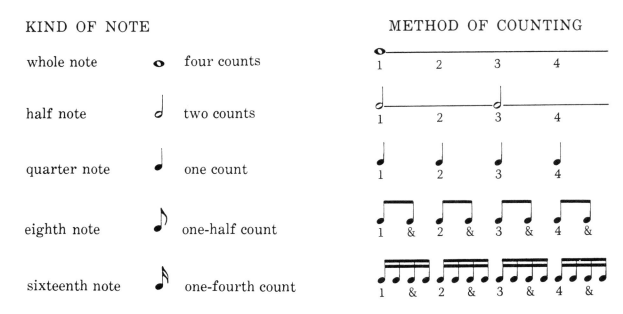

A DOT after a note lengthens its duration by half the value of the note.

The TIME SIGNATURE (also called METER SIGNATURE) looks like a fraction. The upper figure indicates the number of beats or counts in a measure; the lower figure, the kind of note value that receives one count.

EXAMPLE:  **4** = 4 counts to the measure  } There are 4 quarter notes in every measure.
          **4** = the ♩ receives one count  }

A MEASURE is the portion of music enclosed between two bars.

EXAMPLE:

## DIRECTED SELF-STUDY
Clap and count the following note values aloud. The first two rhythm studies in 4/4 time may be counted together by two persons as ensemble practice.

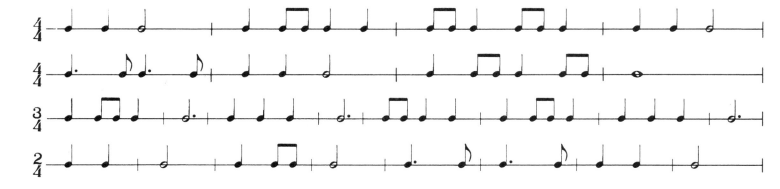

## ALTERNATE RHYTHM PRESENTATION

A less complicated approach to rhythm is suggested for beginners by simply saying note value names, as shown below.

| WHOLE NOTE | DOTTED HALF NOTE | HALF NOTE | DOTTED QUARTER NOTE | QUARTER NOTE | TWO EIGHTH NOTES | FOUR SIXTEENTH NOTES |
|---|---|---|---|---|---|---|
| To be counted: | (Syllables should be spoken in rhythm) | | | | | |
| "Hold that whole note" | "Half note dot" | "Half note" | "Quar-ter dot" | "Quar-ter" | "Two eighths" | "Four six-teenth notes" |

### 3. HOT CROSS BUNS

The rhythmic outline to the old English song, *Hot Cross Buns* is shown below. Clap the beats to this song using this alternate method of counting.

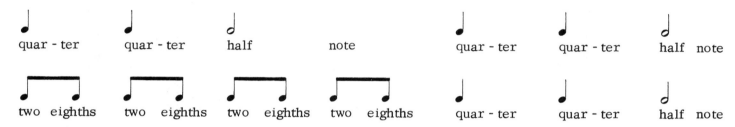

Follow the same practice procedures suggested before: "Play" the song in the air singing the finger numbers aloud. Find the position for both hands. Keep eyes on the book. Play once through singing the finger numbers aloud. Play through a second time counting aloud.

POSITION for HOT CROSS BUNS

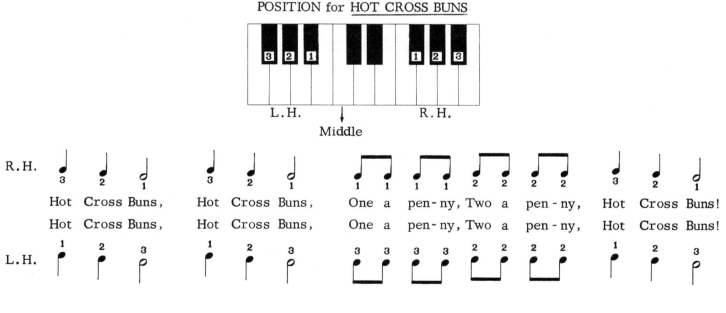

# Unit 2

## THE GROUP I KEYS

> Group 1
> Keys of C,G,F
> Memorize

The Major keys can be divided into four "position-related" groups according to their I or tonic chords.

The Group 1 Keys (C,G,F) have ALL WHITE KEYS in their I or tonic chords. F is underlined because it is the unusual key in this group. The five finger position in F has a black key under the 4th finger in the Right Hand, and under the 2nd finger in the Left Hand.

The circled finger numbers outline the I or tonic chords within the five finger positions below.

### POSITIONS FOR THE GROUP 1 KEYS

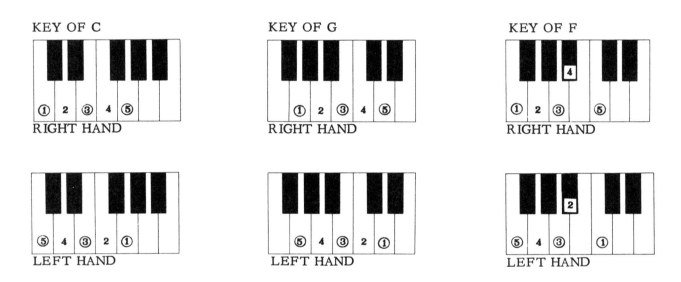

Practice playing the five finger positions (as on p. 3) in the three keys above. Say the letter names of the notes aloud while playing (forward and backward). Do not look at the keyboard while playing. Also play tonic chords for the three keys above.

### RHYTHM DRILLS

Play the rhythm drills below using I chords (either hand). Count aloud while playing. Play by touch; do not look at the keyboard. The first two rhythm drills in 4/4 time may be played together by two persons as ensemble practice.

## THE ARPEGGIO

The ARPEGGIO (from the Italian, *arpeggiare*, to play upon a harp) is a term applied to the notes of a chord when they are played one at a time instead of simultaneously. When playing an arpeggio use the same fingering as the tonic chord, but play one finger at a time. Notice that you must cross hands to get from low to high as pictured on the keyboard below. When crossing hands it is most important to *prepare ahead*. This means that while the Right Hand is playing, the Left Hand is beginning to cross over (preparing ahead) to be in position, ready to play in tempo without hesitation.

"Play" the arpeggio in the air singing the finger numbers aloud. Find the position for both hands. Play once through singing the finger numbers aloud. Play through a second time counting aloud. Begin in the G position (as indicated below), then *transpose* to the keys of C and F.

TRANSPOSE means to play in a different key (to begin at a different pitch) than originally written.

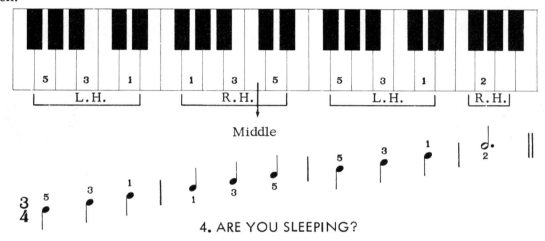

4. ARE YOU SLEEPING?

Sing the melody and play I chords in the key of F, Left Hand; then in the key of G, Right Hand to the song below.

Are You Sleep-ing, Are You Sleep-ing, Broth-er John, Broth-er John?
I                I                I           I

Morn-ing bells are ring-ing, Morn-ing bells are ring-ing, Ding, ding, dong! Ding, ding, dong!
I                I                I           I

Two other songs which may be harmonized with I chords are *Row, Row, Row Your Boat*, and *Three Blind Mice*.

THE ARPEGGIO

4. ARE YOU SLEEPING?

# Unit 2

## SIGHT READING STUDIES

DIRECTED SELF-STUDY
1. Find the position for both hands.
2. Keep eyes on the book.
3. Play legato.
4. Play through first singing the finger numbers aloud.
5. Play through a second time counting aloud.

(i) Position: Key of C  (transpose: Keys of G, F)

(ii) Position: Key of G  (transpose: Keys of F, C)

(iii) Position: Key of F  (transpose: Keys of C, G)

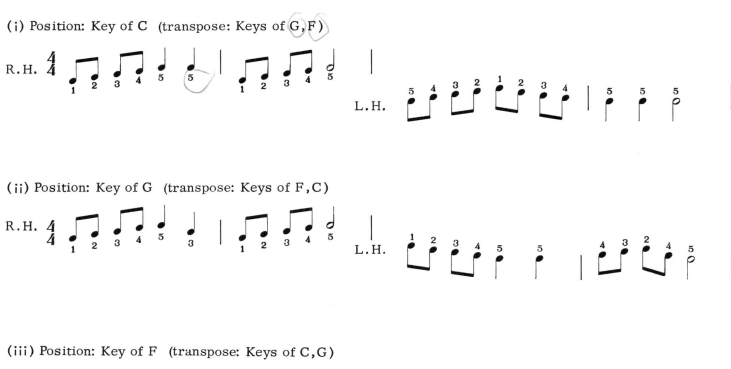

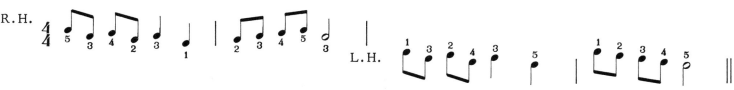

# UNIT 3

- The group 2 keys
- Rhythm drills
- Keyboard review
- Skips and steps on the keyboard

## THE GROUP 2 KEYS

> Group 2
> Keys of D,A,E̲
> Memorize

The Group 2 Keys (D,A,E̲) have a BLACK KEY UNDER THE MIDDLE FINGER and WHITE KEYS ON EITHER SIDE in their I or tonic chords. E is underlined because it is the unusual key in this group. The five finger position in E has TWO black keys under the 2nd and 3rd fingers in the Right Hand, and under the 3rd and 4th fingers in the Left Hand.

The circled finger numbers outline the I or tonic chords within the five finger positions below.

## POSITIONS FOR THE GROUP 2 KEYS

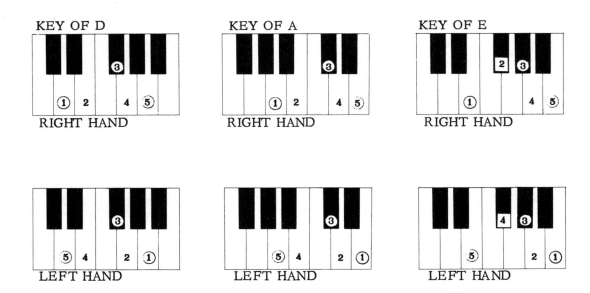

Practice playing the five finger positions (as on p. 3) in the three keys above. Say the letter names of the notes aloud while playing (forward and backward). Do not look at the keyboard while playing. Also play tonic chords for the three keys above, and play arpeggios (as on p. 9).

# Unit 3

## RHYTHM DRILLS

Play the rhythm drills below using I chords (either hand). Count aloud while playing. Play by touch; do not look at the keyboard. The first two rhythm drills in 3/4 time may be played together by two persons as ensemble practice.

## KEYBOARD REVIEW

Write the letter names of the notes marked x.

EXAMPLE:

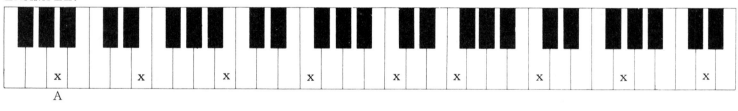

A

Write the letter names of the sharps and flats marked x.

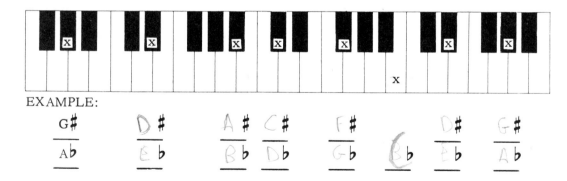

EXAMPLE:

| G♯ | D♯ | A♯ C♯ | F♯ | | D♯ | G♯ |
|---|---|---|---|---|---|---|
| A♭ | E♭ | B♭ D♭ | G♭ | B♭ | E♭ | A♭ |

Write the letter names of the notes in a five finger position for the following keys.

EXAMPLE:

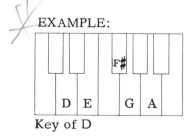

Key of D

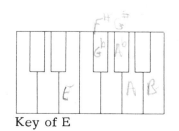

Key of E

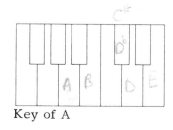

Key of A

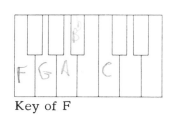

Key of F

## SKIPS AND STEPS ON THE KEYBOARD

Notes move by direction up and down on the music (staff). As preparation for directional reading, think up and down at the keyboard by skips and steps. Note reading will be perceived and transferred to the keyboard with much more facility after having created a mental picture of the keyboard by skip and step drills.

A SKIP skips a finger and skips a letter in the alphabet. A STEP moves from one finger to the next and moves from one alphabet letter to the next.

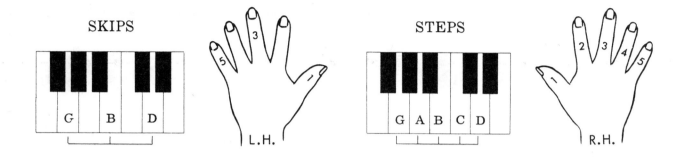

## SKIP AND STEP DRILL

Find the position (either hand). Look only at the music after having found the position. Play the following drills answering each question *aloud*. Add the appropriate sharps or flats. If your answer disagrees with the one given at the end of each exercise, repeat and correct the mistake.

EXAMPLE:

| KEY OF G | KEY OF C | KEY OF F | KEY OF D |
|---|---|---|---|
| 1. Play G | 1. Play C | 1. Play F | 1. Play D |
| 2. Up a step? (A) | 2. Up a skip? ( E ) | 2. Up a step? ( G ) | 2. Up a skip? ( F ) |
| 3. Up a skip? (C) | 3. Up a step? ( F ) | 3. Up a skip? ( D ) | 3. Up a skip? ( A ) |
| 4. Down a step? | 4. Down a skip? | 4. Up a step? | 4. Down a step? |
| (B) | (D) | (C) | (G) |

### 5. GO TELL AUNT RHODIE

Play this song and notice the skips and steps in the melody.

Position: Key of D (transpose: keys of A, E, C)

American Folk Song

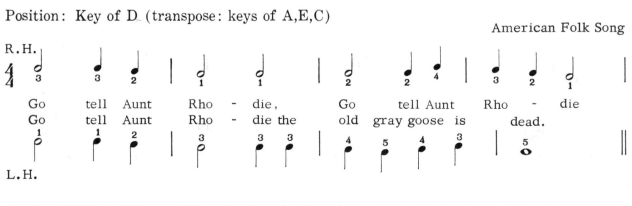

Go    tell Aunt    Rho - die,    Go    tell Aunt    Rho - die
Go    tell Aunt    Rho - die the    old    gray goose is    dead.

GP23

# Unit 3

## SIGHT READING STUDIES

> DIRECTED SELF-STUDY
> 1. Find the position for both hands.
> 2. Keep eyes on the book.
> 3. Play legato.
> 4. Play through first singing the finger numbers aloud.
> 5. Play through a second time counting aloud.

(i) Position: Key of D (transpose: keys of A,E,C)

(ii) Position: Key of A (transpose: keys of D,E,G)

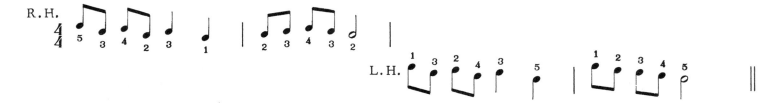

(iii) Position: Key of E (transpose: keys of A,D,F)

Notation

(i)

(ii)

(iii)

# UNIT 4

- The group 3 keys
- Rhythmic notation (6/8 time)
- Skips and steps on the keyboard
- Key (position) review

## THE GROUP 3 KEYS

> Group 3
> Keys of D♭,A♭,E♭
> Memorize

The Group 3 Keys (D♭,A♭,E♭) have a WHITE KEY UNDER THE MIDDLE FINGER and BLACK KEYS ON EITHER SIDE in their I or tonic chords. E♭ is underlined because it is the unusual key in this group. The five finger position in E♭ has TWO white keys under the 2nd and 3rd finger in the Right Hand, and under the 3rd and 4th fingers in the Left Hand.

The circled finger numbers outline the I or tonic chords within the five finger positions below.

## POSITIONS FOR THE GROUP 3 KEYS

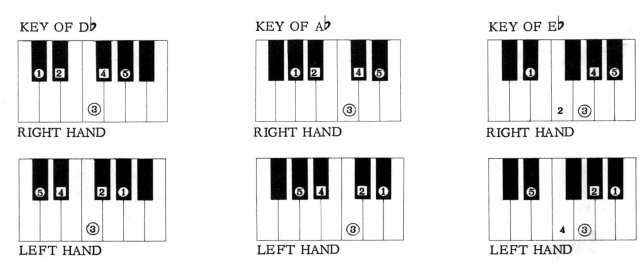

Practice playing the five finger positions (as on p. 3) in the three keys above. Say the letter names of the notes aloud while playing (forward and backward). Do not look at the keyboard while playing. Also play tonic chords for the three keys above, and play arpeggios (as on p. 9).

# Unit 4
## RHYTHMIC NOTATION

(Review) The TIME SIGNATURE (or METER SIGNATURE) looks like a fraction. The upper figure indicates the number of beats or counts in a measure; the lower figure, the kind of note value that receives one count.

EXAMPLE:  6 — 6 counts to the measure

8 — the ♪ receives one count    } There are 6 ♪'s in every measure.

Below are several frequently used kinds of notes found in 6/8 time.
CLAP AND COUNT THEIR NOTE VALUES ALOUD. Accent (>) the first and fourth beats where possible.

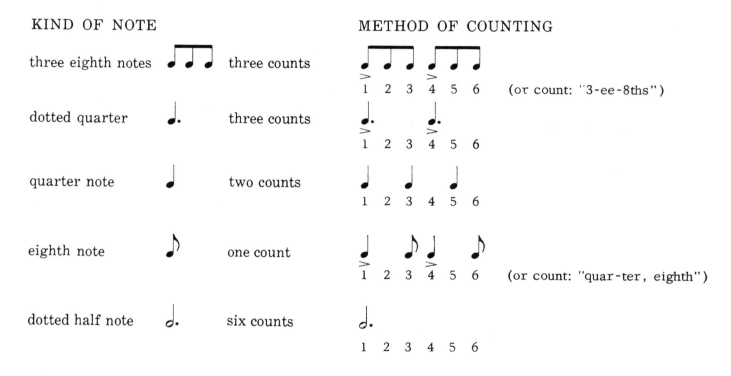

6. ROW, ROW, ROW YOUR BOAT

*Clap* and count note values to this song.

### RHYTHM DRILLS

*Play* the rhythm drills below using I chords (either hand). Count aloud while playing. Play by touch; do not look at the keyboard. All three rhythm drills may be combined by three persons as ensemble practice. Use only one, uniform key for ensemble practice.

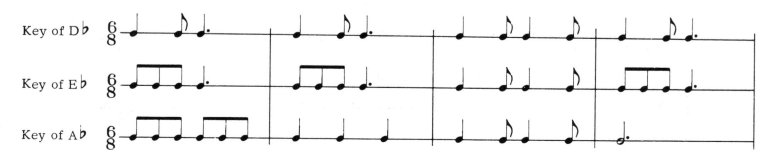

GP23

DIRECTED SELF-STUDY
1. Find the position for both hands.
2. Keep eyes on the book.
3. Play legato.
4. Play through first singing the finger numbers aloud, first with
   the R.H., then with the L.H., finally play both hands together
   in unison.
5. Play through a second time counting aloud.

7. DRINK TO ME ONLY WITH THINE EYES (Excerpt)

Position: Key of C (transpose: Keys of D, D♭)

English Folk Song

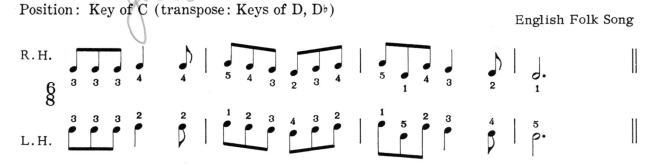

8. ALL THROUGH THE NIGHT (Excerpt)

Be careful with the dotted quarter rhythm. Either count: "1,2 and;" or count "quar-ter dot, eighth." Clap and count the rhythm to this song before playing.

EXAMPLE:

Welsh Folk Song

Count: 1  2 & 3  4    1  2 & 3  4    1  2  3  4 &    1  2  3  4

Position: Key of D (transpose: Keys of G, A♭)

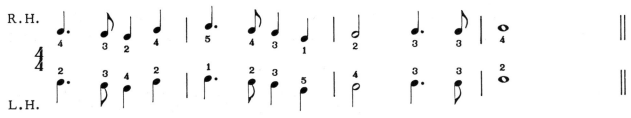

Notation

7. DRINK TO ME ONLY WITH THINE EYES

8. ALL THROUGH THE NIGHT

# Unit 4
## SKIPS AND STEPS ON THE KEYBOARD

Find the position (either hand). Look only at the music after having found the position.
Play the following drills answering each question *aloud*. Add the appropriate sharps or flats.
If your answer disagrees with the one given at the end of each exercise, repeat and correct
the mistake.

| KEY OF G | KEY OF A | KEY OF A♭ | KEY OF C | KEY OF F |
|---|---|---|---|---|
| 1. Play G | 1. Play A | 1. Play A♭ | 1. Play C | 1. Play F |
| 2. Up a skip? | 2. Up a skip? | 2. Up a step? | 2. Up a skip? | 2. Up a skip? |
| 3. Up a skip? | 3. Up a skip? | 3. Down a step? | 3. Up a step? | 3. Up a skip? |
| 4. Down a step? | 4. Down a skip? | 4. Up a skip? | 4. Down a skip? | 4. Down a step? |
| 5. Down a skip? | 5. Up a step? | 5. Up a step? | 5. Up a step? | 5. Down a skip? |
| A | D | D♭ | E | G |

| KEY OF D | KEY OF E♭ | KEY OF C | KEY OF E | KEY OF D♭ |
|---|---|---|---|---|
| 1. Play D | 1. Play E♭ | 1. Play C | 1. Play E | 1. Play D♭ |
| 2. Up a skip? | 2. Up a step? | 2. Up a skip? | 2. Up a step? | 2. Up a skip? |
| 3. Up a step? | 3. Up a skip? | 3. Up a step? | 3. Up a skip? | 3. Down a step? |
| 4. Up a step? | 4. Up a step? | 4. Down a skip? | 4. Down a step? | 4. Up a skip? |
| 5. Down a skip? | 5. Down a skip? | 5. Down a step? | 5. Down a skip? | 5. Down a step? |
| F♯ | G | C | E | F |

## KEY (POSITION) QUIZ

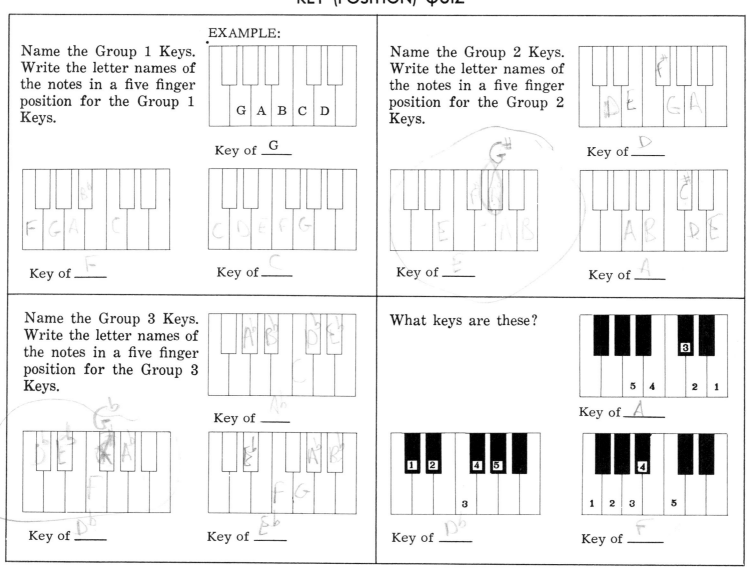

# UNIT 5

- Melody and harmony together
- The five finger position (hands together)
- Melody for hands together (unison)
- Chord quiz

## MELODY AND HARMONY TOGETHER

Nine five finger positions have been presented so far from the three groups of keys. The melody was played first with the Right Hand and then with the Left Hand. Now practice the five finger positions in the three following ways: (i) Play the melody with the Right Hand and the chords with the Left Hand. (ii) Play the melody with the Left Hand and the chords with the Right Hand. (iii) Play the melodies together at the same time in both hands (in unison).

When melody and harmony are played together it is necessary to have the correct *balance* between the two hands. The melody should be predominant and the harmony (accompaniment) subordinate.

Practice the three ways of playing the five finger positions using the study habits already learned: Find the position for both hands. Keep eyes on the book. Play through first singing the finger numbers aloud. Then play through a second time counting aloud.

(i) Position: Any Key from Group 2 (transpose: All other eight Keys)

(ii) Position: Any Key from Group 1 (transpose: All other eight Keys)

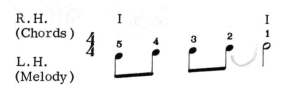 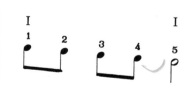

MELODY AND HARMONY TOGETHER

(iii) Position: Any Key from Group 3  (transpose:  All other eight Keys)

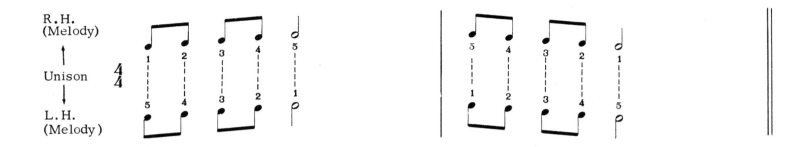

## LEFT HAND MELODY

---

**DIRECTED SELF-STUDY**
1. Find the position for both hands.
2. The L.H. will play the melody, and the R.H. will play I chords.
3. Think of the *balance* between hands; the L.H. should be louder than the R.H.
4. Keep eyes on the book.
5. Play through first singing the finger numbers aloud.
6. Play through a second time counting aloud.

---

Position: Key of D♭ (transpose: A♭, E♭)

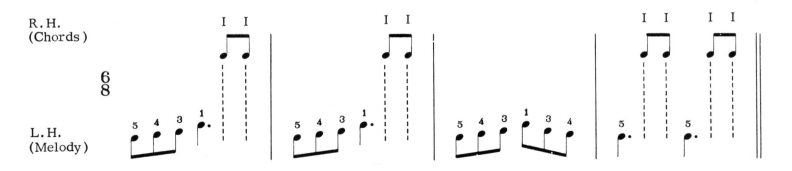

# Unit 5

## 9. THIS OLD MAN

Find the position for both hands. Keep eyes on the book. Play the R.H. melody louder than the L.H. chords (balance). Count aloud while playing.

Position: Key of C (transpose: Keys of D, Ab, A)

English Folk Song

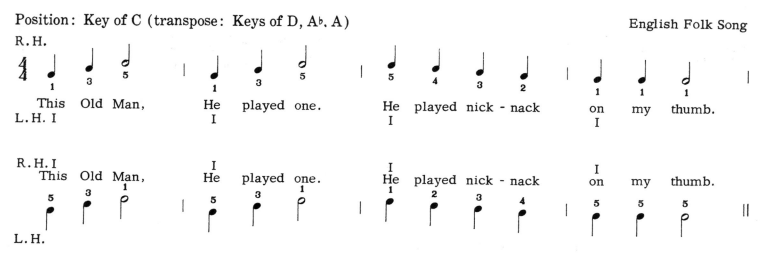

## 10. FRENCH FOLK SONG

This melody is to be played with both hands together at the same time (in unison). After having found the position, keep eyes on the book. Count aloud while playing.

Position: Key of G (transpose: Keys of E, Db, F)

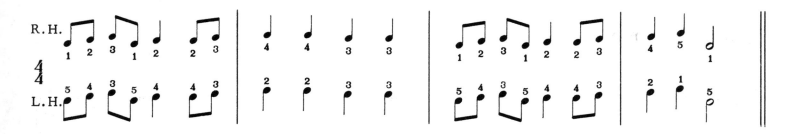

# Unit 5
## RHYTHM DRILLS

Play the rhythm drills below using I chords (either hand). Count aloud while playing. Play by touch; do not look at the keyboard. The first two drills in 4/4 time and the last two drills in 6/8 time may be played together by two persons as ensemble practice. Use only one, uniform key for ensemble practice.

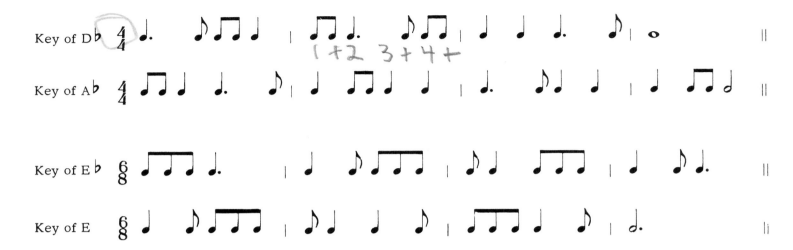

## CHORD QUIZ

Fill in the missing letter names of the notes which will make I Chords. Write the Key of the I Chord. Remember the #'s and ♭'s.

EXAMPLE:

| | | | | |
|---|---|---|---|---|
| 1. | C | E | G | Key of C |
| 2. | D♭ | F | G♯/A♭ | Key of D♭ |
| 3. | D | F♯ | A | Key of D |
| 4. | E♭ | G | B♭ | Key of E♭ |
| 5. | E | A♭/C♯ | B | Key of E |

| | | | | |
|---|---|---|---|---|
| 1. | F | A | C | Key of F |
| 2. | G | B | D | Key of G |
| 3. | A♭ | C | E♭ | Key of A♭ |
| 4. | A | C♯/D♭ | E | Key of A |
| 5. | D | F | A | Key of D |

Fill in the missing finger numbers to make the I Chord, and tell the **KEY** of the Chord.

EXAMPLE:

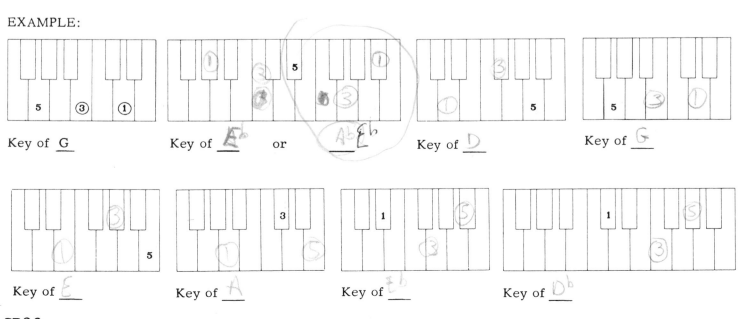

Key of G          Key of E♭  or  A♭ E♭          Key of D          Key of G

Key of E          Key of A          Key of E♭          Key of D♭

# UNIT 6

- The group 4 keys
- The dominant seventh chord
- Melodies harmonized with I and V7 chords
- Review of section one

## THE GROUP 4 KEYS (Unusual Group)

> Group 4
> Keys of G♭,B♭,B
> Memorize

The Group 4 Keys (G♭,B♭,B) have both unusual I chords and five finger positions. Each position and chord must be learned (memorized) individually.

The circled finger numbers outline the I or tonic chords within the five finger positions below.

## POSITIONS FOR THE GROUP 4 KEYS

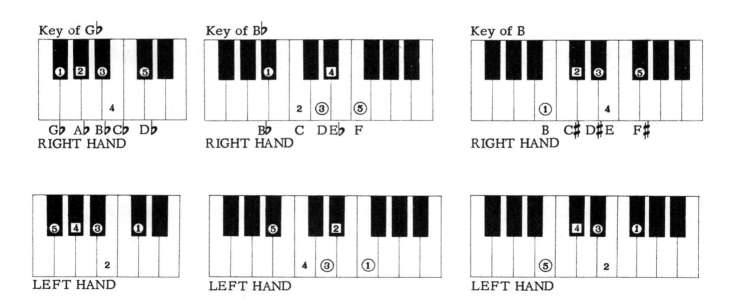

Practice playing the five finger positions (as on p. 3) in the three keys above. Say the letter names of the notes aloud while playing (forward and backward). Do not look at the keyboard while playing. Also play tonic chords for the three keys above, and play arpeggios (as on p. 9).

# Unit 6

### 11. LIGHTLY ROW

German Folk Song

After finding the position for both hands, play and sing the finger numbers aloud, then play and count aloud. Play first the Right Hand, then the Left Hand. Do not look at the keyboard while playing.

Position: Key of G♭ (transpose: Keys of B♭,B,F)

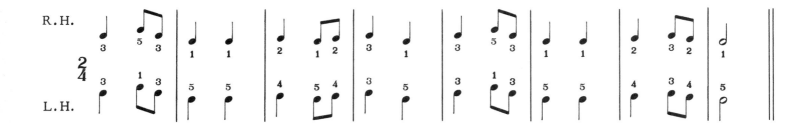

### 12. ENGLISH FOLK SONG

This melody is to be played with both hands together at the same time (in unison). Count aloud while playing. Do not look at the keyboard while playing.

Position: Key of F (transpose: Keys of D,G♭,E)

# Unit 6

## THE DOMINANT SEVENTH CHORD (V₇ Chord)

Many compositions may be harmonized with just two chords: the I (TONIC) chord, and the V7 (DOMINANT SEVENTH) chord. Learn the V7 chord for all keys following the rules below.

To form the V7 chord begin with a I chord position, then:

L.H. Keep 1 the same.
Play 2 (in the five finger position).
Move 5 DOWN the NEAREST key. (The
NEAREST key may be either
black or white.)

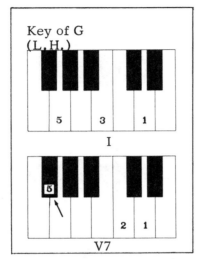
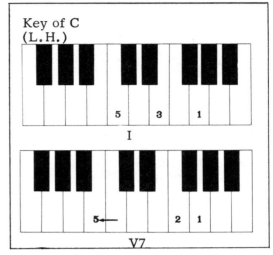

R.H. Keep 5 the same.
Play 4 (in the five finger position).
Move 1 DOWN the NEAREST key. (The
NEAREST key may be either
black or white.)

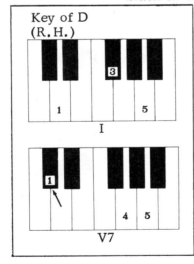
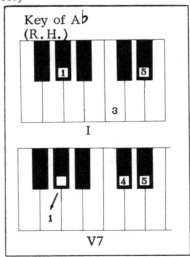

## CHORD DRILLS

Play (I, V7, V7, I) in the following keys.
Play first with the L.H., then with the R.H.

1. Keys of C, G, F
2. Keys of D, A, E
3. Keys of D♭, A♭, E♭
4. Keys of G♭, B♭, B

Play (I, V7, I, V7, I, V7, I) in the following keys. Play first with the L.H., then with the R.H.

1. Keys of C, D, D♭
2. Keys of F, A, A♭
3. Keys of G, E, E♭
4. Keys of G♭, B♭, B

# Unit 6

## I AND V₇ CHORDS COMBINED

Harmonize the following two songs using I and V7 chords as indicated in the music. Before playing each song practice the I and V7 chords for the intended key to get the "feel" of the change in positions. (EXAMPLE: Key of G: Play I, V7, I, V7, I, etc.)

Do not look down at the keyboard when changing chords.

### 13. MERRILY WE ROLL ALONG

Position: Key of G (transpose: Keys of C, F, D)

### 14. THEME FROM BEETHOVEN'S NINTH SYMPHONY

Position: Key of D (transpose: Keys of Db, C, B)

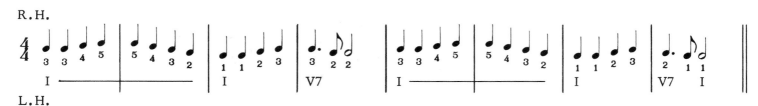

# Unit 6
## REVIEW OF SECTION ONE

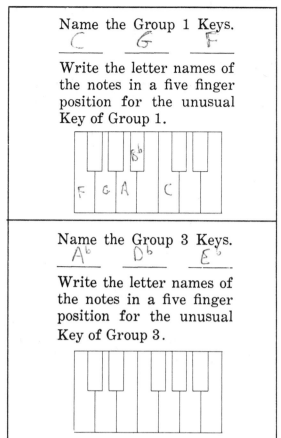

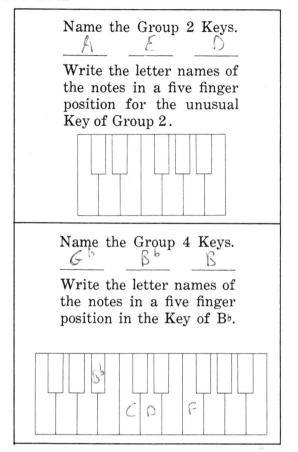

Play the five finger position for all keys chromatically upward. First play in the key of C, then Db,D,Eb,E,F,Gb,G,Ab,A,Bb,B and finally, end on C above middle C. This is the chromatic order of keys on the piano (ascending by half steps).

Also play all the I chords, the arpeggios, and the progression (I, V7, I) chromatically upward in all keys.

## THE CHROMATIC ORDER OF KEYS

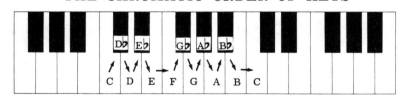

## CHORDS AND RHYTHMS

Play I and V7 Chords in the following keys and rhythms.

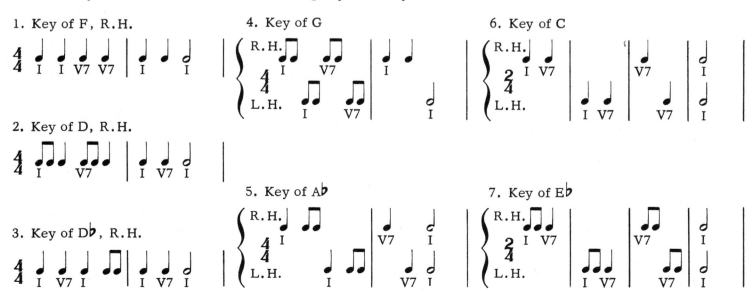

GP23

# SECTION TWO

## READING

ITALIAN HARPSICHORD (17th Century)
Photo courtesy of the Metropolitan Museum of Art, Crosby
Brown Collection of Musical Instruments. This instrument is
carved, gilded and carried on the shoulders of Tritons. Roman
Baroque. 17th Century. The frieze represents the triumph of
Galatea.

# SECTION TWO

## READING

Music reading is the next natural step in the learning process after the pre-reading stage. Here, the keyboard and staff are related to each other. Units seven through thirteen are designed to continue the skills begun in the first six units and to introduce the student to new aspects of keyboard proficiency. Slow, steady progression of reading material is intended for complete student comprehension, and to insure note reading, rather than rote memorizing.

The reading objectives in SECTION TWO include:
1. Learning to play with eyes on the music (playing without visual reference to the keyboard).
2. Reading directionally by intervals (up, down, same), perceiving their relationships on the staff, and transferring them to the keyboard.
3. Learning individual note names and training the ear by singing the notes aloud while playing.
4. Establishing a good rhythmic foundation by counting aloud.
5. Learning to play and hear the I, IV and V7 chords in Major as well as minor by "feel" only, and utilizing chords for harmonizations.

Reading facility is only acquired by constant and continued practice of materials of progressive levels. It is therefore recommended that each line of music assigned be practiced several times per day. After acquiring the sight-reading skills in this section the student is prepared to begin either *Section Three: Functional Piano* or *Section Four: Piano Literature, Technique and Style.*

# UNIT 7

- Musical notation on the grand staff
- Intervals (2nds and 3rds) on the staff
- Sight reading studies
- Review quiz No. 1

## MUSICAL NOTATION ON THE GRAND STAFF

The GRAND STAFF is comprised of two sets of lines and spaces (two staves). Notes are written on the lines and in the spaces, and there are 5 lines and 4 spaces from the lowest to the highest in each staff.

—●— LINE NOTE: The note is placed on the line.

═●═ SPACE NOTE: The note is placed in the space between two lines.

The TREBLE CLEF (or G Clef) 𝄞 sign, encircles the second staff line, locating the first G above middle C, and is the name for the upper half of the Grand Staff. In general, the treble clef sign indicates notes to be played with the right hand from Middle C upward.

Treble Clef

The BASS CLEF (or F Clef) 𝄢 sign, indicates F (fourth staff line) by the dots above and below that line, and is the name for the lower half of the Grand Staff. In general, the bass clef sign indicates notes to be played with the left hand from Middle C downward.

Bass Clef

There are 22 notes that can be written on the Grand Staff without the aid of additional lines drawn. These extra, added lines that can be drawn either below, in the middle, or above the staff, are called LEGER LINES (also spelled ledger).

Memorize the following notes and practice playing them in the correct location on the keyboard. (Note: Flash cards are helpful for learning the names of the notes quickly.)

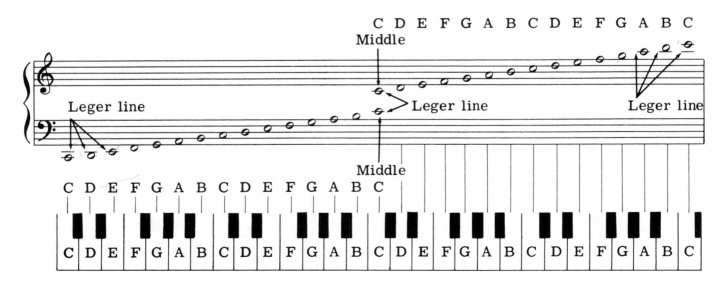

# Unit 7
## NAMING THE LINE NOTES

G is on the bottom line of the Bass Clef. A skip up from G is B, then D, etc. Say all the line notes in order (from low to high) over and over, until they are committed to memory. Remember especially bottom line G in the Bass Clef, and bottom line E in the Treble Clef. These two notes will serve as guides for figuring out the other line notes.

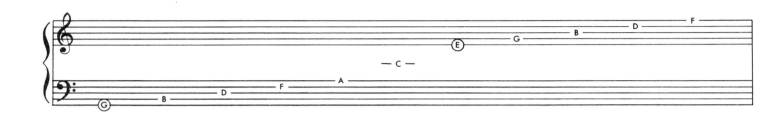

Write the letter names of
the line notes going UP
from the given letter.

Write the letter names of
the line notes going DOWN
from the given letter.

EXAMPLE:

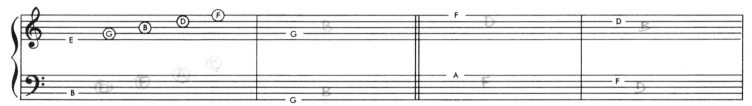

## NAMING THE SPACE NOTES

F is the first space note in the Bass Clef. A skip up from F is A, then C, etc. Say all the space notes in order (from low to high) until they are committed to memory. Remember especially F (the first space note in the Bass Clef) and D (the first space note in the Treble Clef).

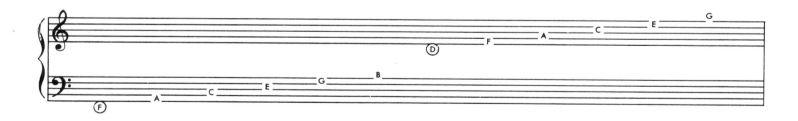

Write the letter names of
the space notes going UP
from the given letter.

Write the letter names of
the space notes going DOWN
from the given letter.

EXAMPLE:

GP23

## NOTE READING AIDS

It is very important to develop good reading habits from the beginning of piano study. Much stress has already been placed on watching the music and not looking down at the keyboard while playing. Now, while reading notes, think by *direction* (up, down, same), and perceive the *distance* between notes.

The distance between two notes is called an *interval*. It is essential to read music by intervals (direction) as well as by individual notes.

The intervals used at present will be: SECONDS (steps) and THIRDS (skips). The other intervals (FOURTHS, FIFTHS) are larger skips and will be presented later.

<table>
<tr>
<td align="center">S T E P<br>(interval of a 2nd)</td>
<td align="center">S K I P<br>(interval of a 3rd)</td>
<td align="center">REPEATED NOTES</td>
</tr>
<tr>
<td>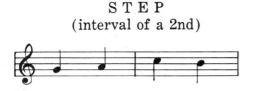</td>
<td>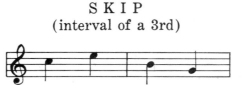</td>
<td></td>
</tr>
<tr>
<td>From a line to a space, or a space to a line is a STEP, or an interval of a 2nd.</td>
<td>From a space to a space, or a line to a line is a SKIP, or an interval of a 3rd.</td>
<td>Repeated notes are either on the same line or space.</td>
</tr>
</table>

## WRITTEN ASSIGNMENT

Draw the note, and write its letter name on the blanks below.

# Unit 7
## SIGHT READING STUDIES

To establish good practice habits follow these recommended practice procedures:

1. Clap and count the rhythm aloud before playing.
2. Find the position for both hands.
3. Keep eyes on the music.
4. Play straight through singing the letter names of the notes aloud.
5. Play through a second time counting the rhythm aloud.

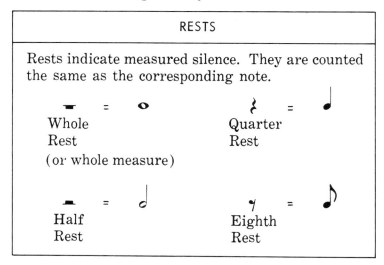

1.

*Key of G (Group 1 key)

whole rest

2.

Key of D (Group 2 key)

## 3. GO TELL AUNT RHODIE

Practice each hand separately, then play both hands in unison.

Key of C

American Folk Song

*Key signatures will be explained later. At present they are used synonymously with position.

# Unit 7
## MELODY WITH RHYTHMIC VARIANCE

Follow the same practice procedures as on p. 32. Notice how the
rhythm changes in the reading studies on this page. The same
melody, however, is used throughout.*

*These melodies may be played with both hands together in unison as p. 32, No. 3.

# Unit 7

## SIGHT READING IN DIFFERENT PIANO REGISTERS

Study the melodies below before playing them to determine where to place your hands on the keyboard. Notice the changes in clef signs in numbers 9 and 11. Clef changes are used primarily to facilitate reading either low or high registers at the keyboard, and to eliminate excessive use of leger lines.

Read the leger lines in the positions below by intervals (skips and steps). Follow the same practice procedures as on p. 32.

## SHIFTING REGISTERS AND METER CHANGES

Certain melodies require changes of meter into irregular groupings, as in No. 13. (EXAMPLE: 3/4, 4/4, etc.)

Melodies may also appear in odd-numbered time signatures, as in
No. 14. (EXAMPLE: 5/4, 9/8)

12.

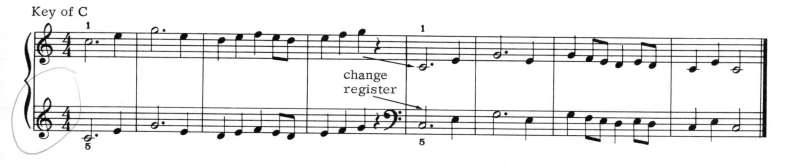

13.

14.

# Unit 7
## REVIEW QUIZ NO. I

I.  Write the letter names of the notes on the blanks below.

EXAMPLE:

<u>E</u>   <u>D</u>   <u>F</u>   <u>B</u>   <u>D</u>   <u>G</u>        ___  ___  ___  ___  ___  ___

II.  Draw the indicated note on the staff above each letter.

EXAMPLE:

E   G   D   A   C   F   B        A   C   D   F   B   G   E

III.  SKIP AND STEP DRILL

Begin with the key note and write the answers to the following questions.  Do this away from the keyboard and "picture" the positions in your mind.  Remember the sharps and flats.

EXAMPLE:

KEY OF D♭
1.  Up a skip?  <u>F</u>
2.  Up a step?  <u>G♭</u>
3.  Down a skip?  <u>E♭</u>
4.  Up a step?  <u>F</u>

KEY OF C
1.  Up a skip?  ___
2.  Up a skip?  ___
3.  Down a step?  ___
4.  Down a skip?  ___

KEY OF G
1.  Up a skip?  ___
2.  Up a skip?  ___
3.  Down a step?  ___
4.  Down a skip?  ___

KEY OF A♭
1.  Up a step?  ___
2.  Up a skip?  ___
3.  Down a step?  ___
4.  Down a step?  ___

IV.  Answer the following questions.

EXAMPLE:
1.  The treble clef is also called the  <u>G</u>  clef.
2.  The bass clef is also called the ___ clef.
3.  _____ lines may be written above, below, or in the middle of the Grand Staff.
4.  ___ is the bottom line in the bass clef and ___ is the top line in the treble.
5.  There are ___ line and space notes that may be drawn on the Grand Staff.

V.  Play I and V7 chords in the chord drill below.  Count aloud.  Do not look at your hands while changing chords.

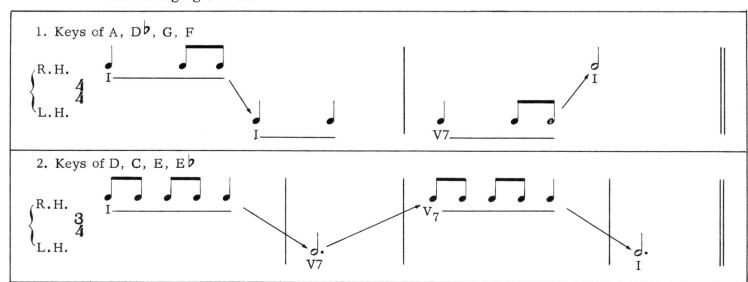

# UNIT 8

- Minor chords and positions
- Sight reading studies
- The order of sharps and sharp key signatures
- Intervals of 4ths and 5ths
- Notation of chords (Major, minor, V7)
- Review quiz No. 2

## MINOR CHORDS AND POSITIONS

To play a minor five finger position (or a minor I chord), begin with a MAJOR POSITION and move the middle finger down one half step (the nearest key down). The nearest key down may be either black or white.

Play the following chords.

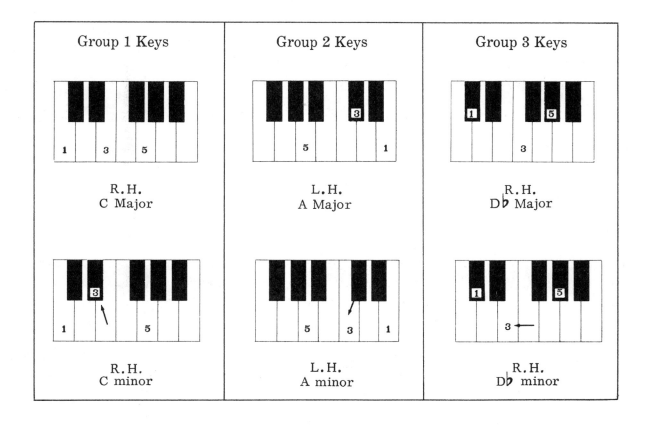

Play Major (M) and minor (m) chords in the following keys and rhythms; use either hand. Play these chords by "feel"; keep eyes on the book while playing.

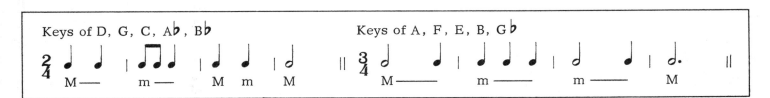

# Unit 8
## SIGHT READING STUDIES

Find the position for both hands. Keep eyes on the book. Play
legato. Play once through singing the letter names of the notes
aloud. Play through a second time counting aloud.

*Minor key signatures will be explained later. At present they are used synonymously with position.

# Unit 8
## THE ORDER OF SHARPS

The SHARPS are always written in the same order on the staff.
*Memorize* this sequence.

Line Sharp                                                                                   Space Sharp

F C G D A E B

*Fuzzy Cats Get Dirty After Every Bath*

Write the order of sharps four times on the staff below.

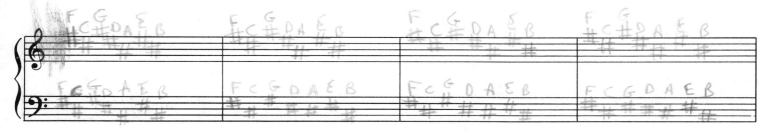

## KEY SIGNATURES OF MAJOR KEYS (Sharps)

The KEY SIGNATURE at the beginning of each staff indicates
two things:

1. The notes to be sharped (or flatted) throughout the entire
   composition.
2. The main key (tonic key) of the composition.

The key signature (tonic key) will be found in Major SHARP
keys by thinking one note above the last sharp.

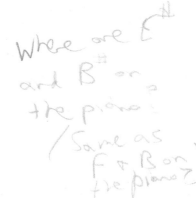

*Where are E♯
and B♯ on
the piano?
(Same as
F ♮ B on
the piano?)*

EXAMPLES:

Key of G          Key of A          Key of D

Name the key.

EXAMPLE:

G     E     B     D     F♯     A     C♯

A     D     E     F♯     B     G     C♯

# Unit 8
## SIGHT READING STUDIES

Find the position for both hands.  Keep eyes on the book.  Play
legato.  Sing the names of the notes aloud.  Count aloud.

## INTERVALS OF FOURTHS AND FIFTHS

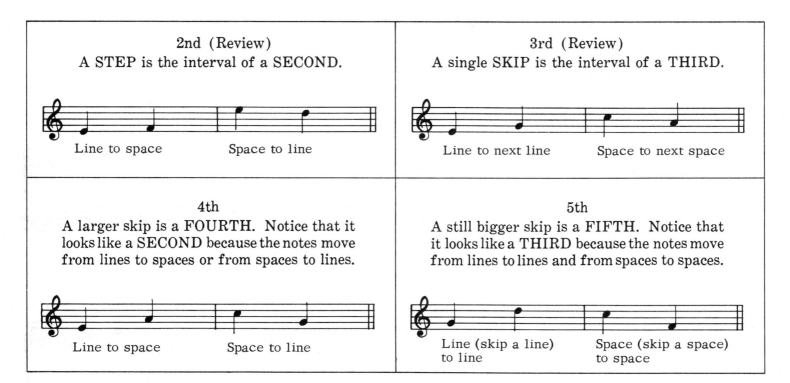

Name the following intervals.

EXAMPLES:

3rd    4th    ___  ___  ___  ___  ___  ___

Name the intervals used in the following two compositions (Nos. 25 and 26).

### 25.

Key of_____

### 26. ARE YOU SLEEPING?

Notice the slight change in position in the Right Hand.

Key of_____

English

# Unit 8
## SIGHT READING STUDIES

Sing the letter names of the notes aloud. Count aloud. Practice
numbers 30 and 31 HANDS SEPARATELY at first, then play
as written.

Name the intervals used in the following compositions.

27. RUSSIAN FOLK SONG

Key of G minor

28.

Key of C Major

change
register

29.

Key of _____

30.

Key of _____

31.

Key of C Major

## CHORD NOTATION

Play the following chords, first HANDS SEPARATELY, then together.

**MAJOR-MINOR CHORDS**

The NATURAL sign (♮) is used to cancel either a sharp or flat.

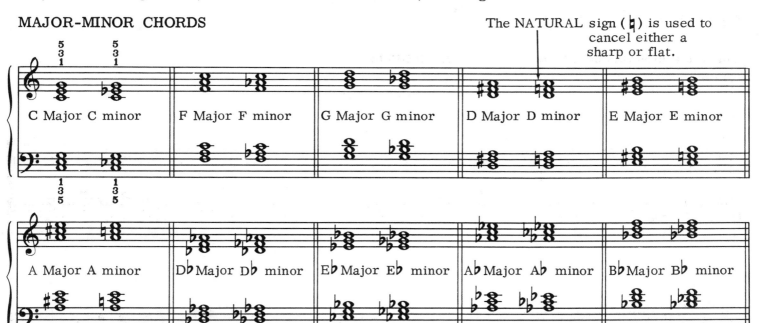

The DOUBLE FLAT (♭♭) lowers a note one whole step.

**ENHARMONIC CHORDS**

ENHARMONIC notes have the same sound but different spellings — as in English, to, too, two. The G♭ Major and minor chord is often spelled F♯ Major and minor, and D♭ Major and minor is often spelled C♯ Major and minor.

## I and V7 CHORDS (TONIC AND DOMINANT SEVENTH CHORDS)

The <u>same</u> V7 chord is used for both Major and minor chords.

C Major          C minor

EXAMPLE:

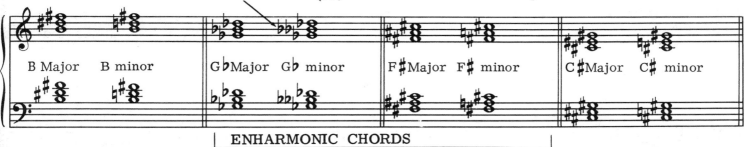

Play the following I and V7 chords with the Left Hand. Play them also in minor.

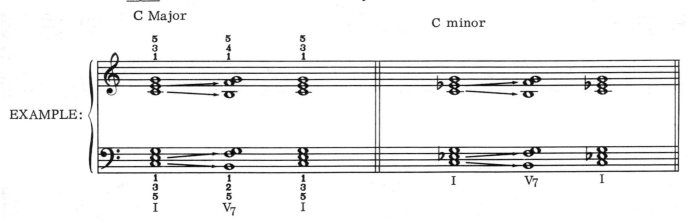

# Unit 8
## THE FIVE FINGER PATTERN HARMONIZED
## WITH I and V-7 CHORDS

### (To be learned in all keys)

IMPORTANT PRACTICE REMINDERS: Play the five finger patterns in the two exercises below using a legato touch. Be careful of the *balance* between the melody and harmony (play the chords softer than the moving notes). Think ahead for each new chord change. Do not look at the keyboard while playing, but rather "feel" for each new chord change.

(i) *

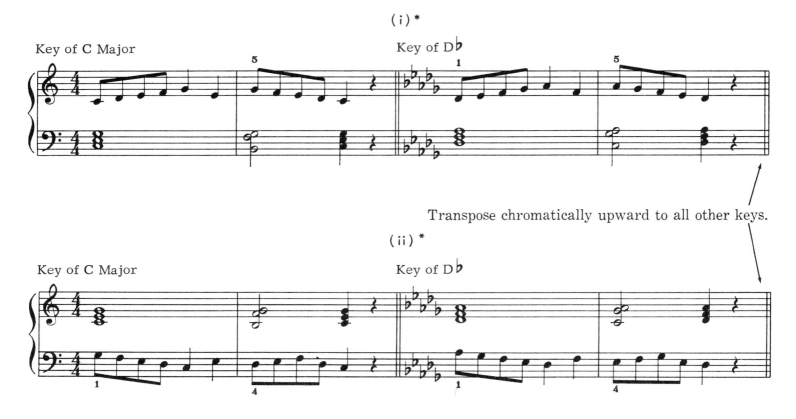

Transpose chromatically upward to all other keys.

(ii) *

### 32. MERRILY WE ROLL ALONG

Play I, V7, I, V7, I in the key of this song before beginning to play it as written.

Key of _____ (Transpose to other keys. Also play in minor.)

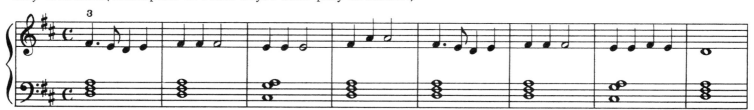

**C**—*(common time)* 4 beats to the measure *(4/4)*

*These two exercises may be practiced in minor positions in addition to the Major notated above.

A melody frequently begins on an "off" beat (a beat other than the first in the measure). Such a melody would begin with an UPBEAT (sometimes called a PICKUP), as opposed to a regular melody that would begin on the DOWNBEAT (first beat in the measure).

If a melody begins with an upbeat there will be an irregular number of counts in the final measure, called an INCOMPLETE MEASURE.

Play I, V7, I, V7, I in the keys of these songs before beginning to play them.

## 33. THE ERIE CANAL

Key of D minor (Transpose to other keys.)

W. S. Allen

## 34. LEFT HAND MELODY

Key of _____ (Transpose to other keys. Also play in minor.)

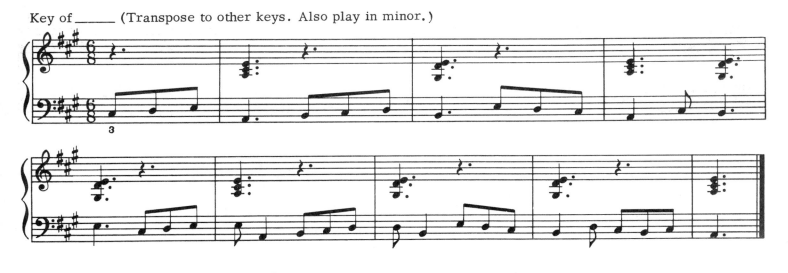

## 35. LIGHTLY ROW

Key of F Major (Transpose to other keys. Also play in minor.)

German Folk Song

46

# Unit 8

## REVIEW QUIZ No. 2

I. Draw the following notes in the correct location on the staff (or on leger lines).

EXAMPLE:

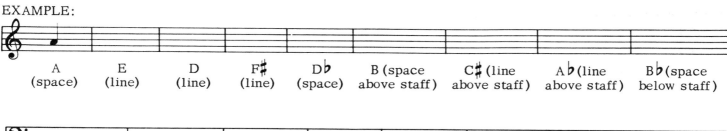

A (space)   E (line)   D (line)   F♯ (line)   D♭ (space)   B (space above staff)   C♯ (line above staff)   A♭ (line above staff)   B♭ (space below staff)

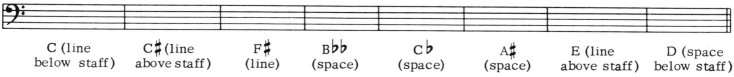

C (line below staff)   C♯ (line above staff)   F♯ (line)   B♭♭ (space)   C♭ (space)   A♯ (space)   E (line above staff)   D (space below staff)

II. Identify the following intervals.

EXAMPLE:

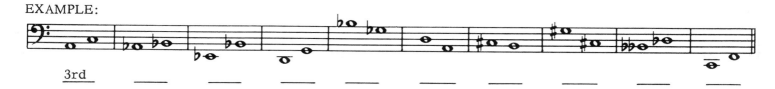

3rd

III. Identify the following Major key signatures.

EXAMPLE:

D

IV. Write tonic chords in the following keys.

EXAMPLE:

A Major   E Major   E minor   G Major   G minor   D♭ Major   D minor   F Major

V. Write the chord progression I, V7, I in the following keys.

EXAMPLE:

G Major   C Major   F Major   D Major   D minor

GP23

# Unit 9

- The tie, slur, phrase
- Sight reading studies
- The order of flats and flat key signatures
- Staccato touch
- Duets
- Review quiz No. 3

The song below is presented in three different versions: first in unison, then in two voices (or parts), then harmonized with I and V7 chords. Count aloud while playing these three versions.

ENGLISH FOLK SONG
36-A (Unison)

Key of _____

36-B (Two Voices)

Key of C Major

36-C (Harmonized)

Key of _____

GP23

# Unit 9

## TIED NOTES

A TIE is a curved line which connects two notes of the same pitch (either two line or two space notes). The second note is not played again, but is held and counted for its full value.

EXAMPLES:

## SLURRED NOTES

A SLUR is a curved line (either above or below a group of two or more notes) which indicates that these notes are to be played as a group and are to be legato. Usually the first note of a slurred group is slightly stressed and the last note of the group is slightly softened. It is helpful to say the words "DOWN-UP" when playing slurs at the piano, because the wrist will be down (lower) for the first note and up (higher) for the last note.

EXAMPLES:

## EXERCISES FOR WRIST FLEXIBILITY

Say the words "DOWN-UP" aloud while playing, changing your wrist position from low to high. Practice first HANDS SEPARATELY, then together. Transpose chromatically upward to all other keys.

(i)

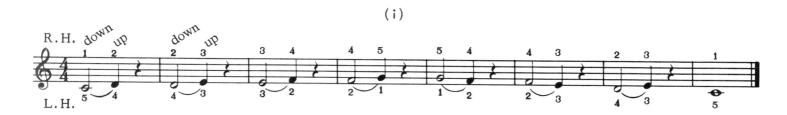

(ii)

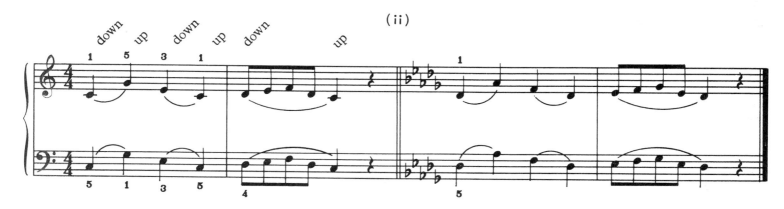

## THE PHRASE

A musical PHRASE is a structural grouping of several measures into a basic unit which is comparable to a line of poetry or a sentence in English. Phrases usually fall into regular groupings of four or eight measures. There should be a "breath" at the end of each phrase as if the melody were sung rather than played. Within a long phrase there may be a number of slurred groupings, but these correspond to the natural rise and fall of the melodic line, and are only smaller units within a longer thought.

When playing the four studies below, lift your hands slightly at the end of each little slur (with a down-up wrist motion), and slower (longer) at the ends of the phrases as if taking a breath.

## SIGHT READING PHRASES CONTAINING SLURRED GROUPINGS

Key of _____ 37.

PHRASE 1 PHRASE 2

₵–(alla breve) 2 strong beats to the *measure* (2/2)

Key of F Major 38.

PHRASE 1

PHRASE 2

Key of _____ 39.

PHRASE 1 PHRASE 2

Key of _____ 40.

PHRASE 1 PHRASE 2

# Unit 9
## SIGHT READING STUDIES IN MINOR KEYS

When playing each of the studies on this page, think ahead for
any changes in hand positions that might occur.  Play straight
through looking far enough ahead to keep going in tempo.

Play I, V7, I, V7, I in the keys of these songs before beginning to
play them.

## THE ORDER OF FLATS

The FLATS are always written in the same order on the staff.
*Memorize* this sequence.

Line Flat    B  E  A  D  G  C  F    Space Flat

*Bead Great Chicago Fire*

Write the order of flats four times on the staff below.

## KEY SIGNATURES OF MAJOR KEYS (Flats)

The KEY SIGNATURE at the beginning of each staff indicates
two things:

1.  The notes to be flatted (or sharped) throughout the entire
    composition.
2.  The main key (tonic key) of the composition.

The key signature (tonic key) will be found in Major FLAT keys
by thinking the next-to-the-last flat.

EXAMPLES:                                          EXCEPTIONS:

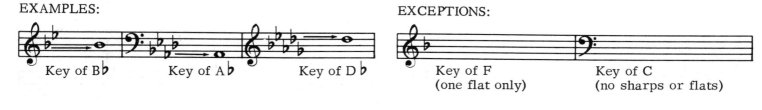

Key of B♭        Key of A♭        Key of D♭        Key of F              Key of C
                                                   (one flat only)       (no sharps or flats)

Name the key.

EXAMPLE:

B♭   ___   ___   ___   ___   ___   ___

___   ___   ___   ___   ___   ___   ___

# Unit 9

STACCATO touch is the opposite of legato. Staccato notes are disconnected tones as opposed to smooth and connected tones in legato playing. Staccato touch is indicated by a dot either above or below the note head.

EXAMPLE:

## EXERCISE: STACCATO STUDY

Play the study below in all keys transposing chromatically upward.

D.C. AL FINE means to return to the beginning (Da Capo — the "head") and repeat to Fine (pronounced — Fee-nay), the end or final repose.

### 45. ALOUETTE

French Folk Song

Key of _____

A - lou - et - te    gen - tille  A - lou - et - te,    A - lou - et - te    je  te  plu - me - rai.

Fine

Je  te  plu - me - rai la  tete,    je  te  plu - me - rai la  tete,    Et  la  tete, et  la  tete,    et  la  tete, oh

D.C. al Fine

Key of _____

### 46. STACCATO MARCH

☰ — repeat sign

## FINGER EXERCISES

Play the exercises below in all keys transposing chromatically upward. Play once through all *legato*, then play through a second time all *staccato*.

# Unit 9

## 47. UNISON
### (No. 1 from "The First Term at the Piano")

Béla Bartók
(1881-1945)

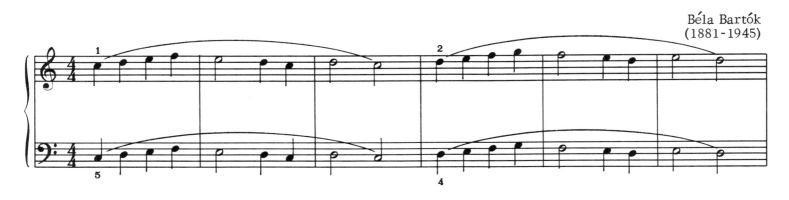

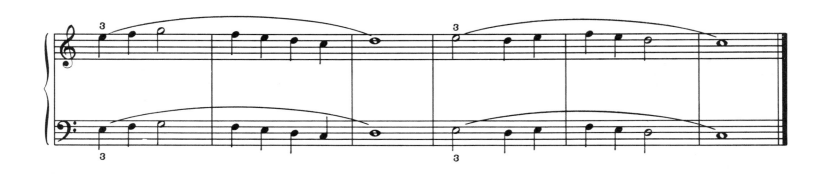

## 48. A DUET
### (No. 2 from "The First Term at the Piano")

Béla Bartók

# Unit 9

55

## RAPID READING

Play the eight single line melodies below either singing the note names aloud or counting aloud. Find each new position as quickly as possible. Observe the key signatures, clef signs, ties, slurs, and rests. *

*All the melodies on this page may be played with both hands at the same time in unison.

GP23

# Unit 9

### 49. DUET
*Secondo

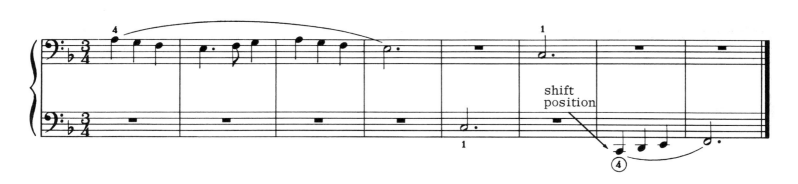

### 50. DUET
Secondo

### 51. DUET
Secondo

### 52. DUET
Secondo

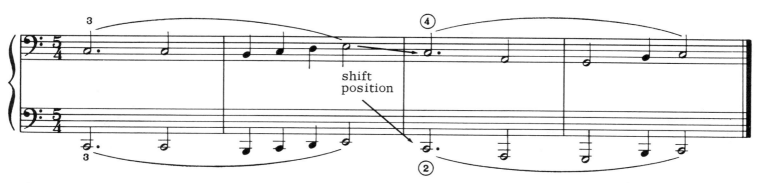

*SECONDO — the second player's part.

# Unit 9

### 49. DUET
*Primo

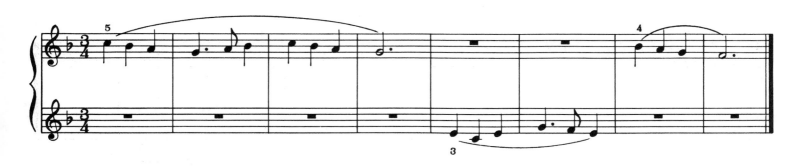

### 50. DUET
Primo

### 51. DUET
Primo

### 52. DUET
Primo

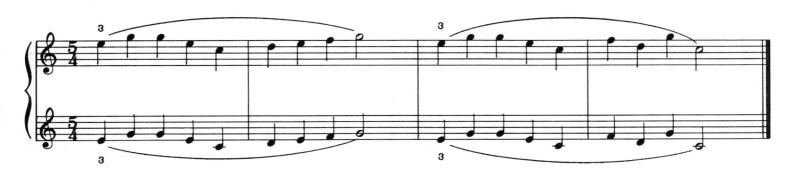

*PRIMO — the first player's part.

# Unit 9

## REVIEW QUIZ NO. 3

I.  Write in the missing letters which spell either a Major or minor five finger position.
    Do this away from the keyboard.  Remember the sharps and flats.
    EXAMPLE:

1.  C (D) (E♭) (F) G      minor
2.  D ___ ___ ___ A      Major
3.  E♭ ___ ___ ___ ___      minor
4.  ___ A♭ ___ ___ D♭      Major

5.  ___ C♯ ___ ___ F♯      Major
6.  A♭ ___ ___ ___ E♭      minor
7.  ___ ___ B♭ ___ ___      Major
8.  ___ ___ F ___ ___      Major

II. Answer the following questions.
    EXAMPLE:

1.  A __tie__ is a curved line which connects notes on the same line or space.
2.  Slurs begin with a _____ wrist position and end with an _____ wrist position.
3.  A phrase is a _____ _____ and is comparable to a line of poetry.
4.  This sign, :‖ is called a _____ _____.

III. Write the order of sharps and flats on the staff below.

SHARPS                  FLATS

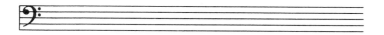

IV. Identify the following Major key signatures.

EXAMPLE:

D

# UNIT 10

- Playing out of the five finger position
- The subdominant chord
- Reading studies out of the five finger position
- Duets
- Review quiz No. 4

## SHIFTING HAND POSITIONS

Playing out of the five finger position will require moving either one finger or a number of fingers or even a "shift" of the entire hand position. In the two examples below the shift of hand position is indicated by a vertical line: | . This line will indicate a quick change to a new hand position temporarily, then a return to the original position will be indicated by the following line.

Count aloud while playing, and try to anticipate the shift in hand position so there is no delay in the rhythm.

53. WALTZ

Key of_____

54. MARCH

Key of_____

# Unit 10
## EXERCISES FOR CHANGING FINGER POSITIONS

Practice these studies first HANDS SEPARATELY, then together. Transpose to all keys.

(i) EXTENSION (above)

(ii) EXTENSION (below)

(iii) CONTRACTION

(iv) TURNING (under)  CROSSING (over)

*NO. 1 from "The Virtuoso Pianist"
(finger extension study)

Charles Louis Hanon
(1820-1900)

*The original version has a two octave range and is notated in
sixteenth notes.

# Unit 10

A HALF STEP (half tone) moves from one key to the next nearest key on the piano, and is explained as a minor second in theory.

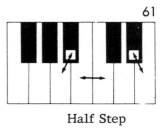

Half Step

A WHOLE STEP (whole tone) moves from one key to the next key with one key in between. A whole step is actually a combination of two half steps, and is explained as a major second in theory.

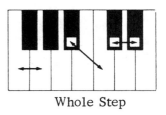

Whole Step

## THE SUBDOMINANT CHORD (IV Chord)

Numerous compositions may be harmonized with the three primary chords: the I (TONIC) chord, the V7 (DOMINANT SEVENTH) chord, and the IV (SUBDOMINANT) chord. Learn the IV chord for all keys following the rules below.

To form the IV chord begin with a I chord position, then:

| L.H. | Keep 5 the same. Play 2 (in the five finger position). Move 1 UP a WHOLE STEP. | R.H. | Keep 1 the same. Move 3 UP a HALF STEP. Move 5 UP a WHOLE STEP. |

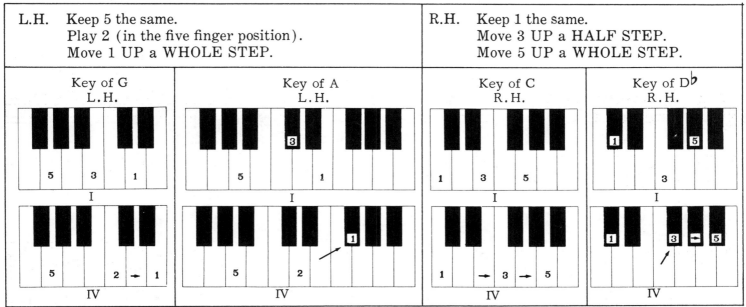

Play the chord progression I, IV, I for all keys. Do not look at your hands, but rather "feel" for each new change, and anticipate the new chord before playing it. Play HANDS SEPARATELY at first (L.H., then R.H.), then combine both hands.

## CHORD PROGRESSION DRILL

Play the chord progressions below following the suggestions above. Learn this pattern for all keys.

## RHYTHM DRILL

Play the chords in the following keys. Count aloud while playing. Keep eyes on the book.

Keys of C, D, A♭, E, F, G

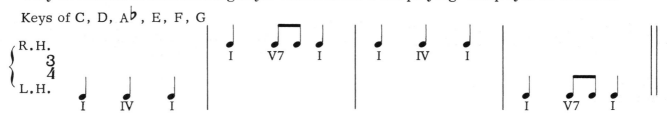

GP23

# Unit 10

An interval of a SIXTH is a large skip requiring either an extension of the thumb or 5th finger out of the five finger position.

EXAMPLES:

### 55. LAVENDER'S BLUE

Old English Folk Song

Key of _____

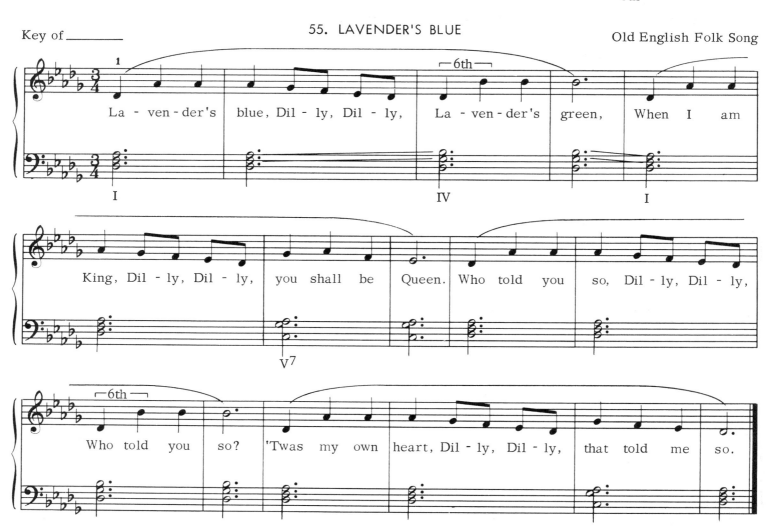

La - ven-der's blue, Dil - ly, Dil - ly, La - ven-der's green, When I am

King, Dil - ly, Dil - ly, you shall be Queen. Who told you so, Dil - ly, Dil - ly,

Who told you so? 'Twas my own heart, Dil - ly, Dil - ly, that told me so.

The FERMATA is a sign meaning to pause or hold longer than the time value of the note.

### 56. FOR HE'S A JOLLY GOOD FELLOW

English Song
(fermata)

Key of _____

finger extension

finger extension

Fine

D.C. al Fine

finger extension

finger extension

## SIGHT READING SUGGESTIONS

1. Analyze the composition before beginning to play it through. Check the key and time signatures, rhythm patterns, slurs, ties, and rests. Look through to see where the shifts in hand positions will occur. (Circle the shifts in hand positions for the song below.)

2. Read by patterns in units, rather than by individual note by note sequence.

3. Listen carefully to perceive the harmonic changes.

4. Constantly look ahead to comprehend new patterns before actually playing them.

### 57. YANKEE DOODLE

Traditional

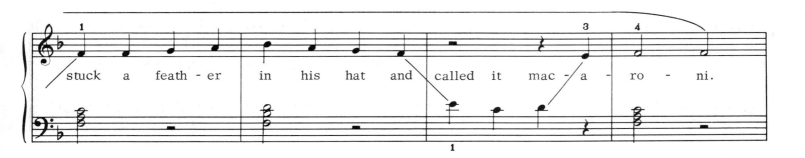

(Notice that the top note of
the IV chord is missing.)

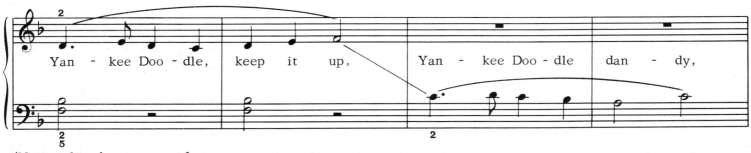

# Unit 10

## RAPID READING STUDIES
## EMPHASIZING SHIFTING POSITIONS

Read straight through each of the three studies on this page.
Think ahead for the changes in positions, and look far enough
ahead to keep going in tempo. Notice that these three songs are
variations on well-known melodies. All three may be transposed
to other keys.

### 58.

### 59.

### 60.

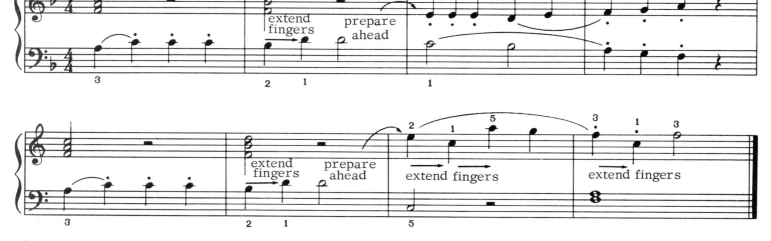

An ACCIDENTAL is an added sharp, flat, or natural which is written immediately before a note and affects only the staff degree on which it is written. The duration for the accidental is for one measure only, and must be re-written if used in subsequent measures.

Mark the changes in hand positions for the two songs below.

61.

Key of C minor

62.

Key of A minor

# Unit 10

### 63. ARE YOU SLEEPING?
Duet
Secondo

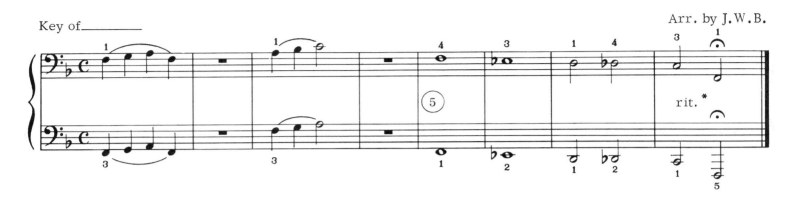

### 64. THE THUNDERER
Duet
Secondo

John Philip Sousa (1854-1932)
Arr. by J.W.B.

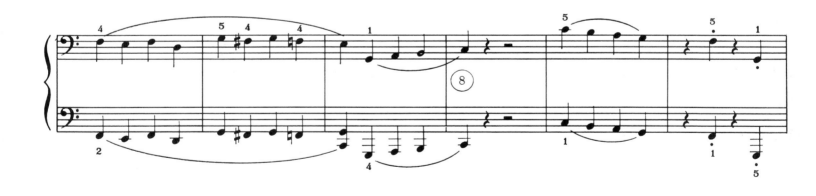

*Ritardando (rit.) see p. 76 for explanation.

## 63. ARE YOU SLEEPING?
Duet
Primo

Key of _____

Arr. by J.W.B.

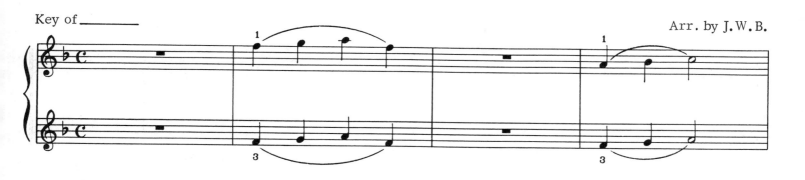

## 64. THE THUNDERER
Duet
Primo

Key of _____

John Philip Sousa (1854-1932)
Arr. by J.W.B.

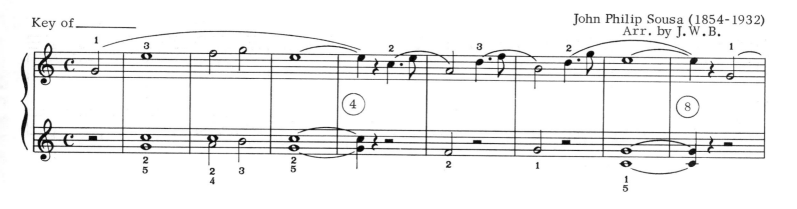

*Ritardando (rit.) see p. 76 for explanation.

# Unit 10

## REVIEW QUIZ No. 4

I. Write in the missing letters which spell IV chords, and name the key to which it belongs. (The first letter of the chord is the key note.)

EXAMPLE:

1. _C_ F _A_ IV chord in _C_     5. ___ G ___ IV chord in ___
2. ___ B♭ ___ IV chord in ___     6. ___ ___ F♯ IV chord in ___
3. ___ ___ E IV chord in ___     7. ___ A ___ IV chord in ___
4. ___ E♭ ___ IV chord in ___     8. ___ ___ C IV chord in ___

II. Answer the following questions.

EXAMPLE:

1. Playing out of a five finger position will require either finger __extension__ or __contraction__.
2. A _____ _____ moves from one key to the next nearest key.
3. This sign, ⌢ is called a _____ and means _____.
4. D.C. al fine means _____.
5. Fine means _____.
6. An accidental is an added _____, _____, or _____.
7. A _____ _____ is a combination of two half steps.

III. Identify the following intervals.

EXAMPLE:

4th ___ ___ ___ ___ ___ ___ ___ ___

IV. Write the chord progression I, IV, I in the following keys.

EXAMPLE:

C Major          D Major          G Major          A♭ Major          F Major

V. Write the chord progression I, IV, I, V7, I in the following keys.

EXAMPLE:

D Major                    F Major                    G Major

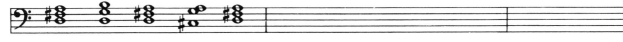

# Unit 11

- Musical form (ABA)
- Tempo, dynamics
- Major scales, beginning on white keys
- Sight reading studies, shifting hand positions
- Syncopated rhythm
- Duets
- Review quiz No. 5

The song *Oh! Susanna* uses sixteenth notes in its melody. Since this particular song is well known, the sixteenth notes could be played by "ear." For thorough understanding however, practice clapping the rhythm study below for various ways of grouping sixteenth notes. (One person clap the top line and another clap the bottom line for ensemble practice.)

65. OH! SUSANNA

Stephen Foster
(1826 - 1864)

# Unit II
## FORM IN MUSIC

Music is constructed of melody, rhythm, and harmony. These elements are so designed architecturally that they fit into some kind of MUSICAL FORM. One of the simplest musical forms occurs when there is a statement, digression, and repeat of the original statement. This is generally referred to as THREE-PART SONG FORM, or A B A FORM (very often, however: A A¹ B A¹).

An analysis of the song below:

A —first line (the first complete musical phrase)

A¹—second line (repeat of line one, generally referred to as A¹)

B —third line (contrasting material, or phrase)

A¹—fourth line (repeat of original statement — line two)

An understanding of similar or dissimilar phrases will enhance the learning process, therefore, analyze all subsequent compositions for formal structure.

Mark the changes in hand positions.

Key of _____

66. DID YOU EVER SEE A LASSIE?

Scottish Folk Song

TEMPO means the rate of speed at which a composition should be played. The intrinsic character of the music usually suggests the tempo, but most composers generally indicate the rate of speed (in Italian words). A complete listing of all tempos is given in the Dictionary in the appendix at the back of the book on p. 209. Some of the more frequently used tempos are listed here.

Largo — broadly, very slowly
Andante — slowly, but flowing along
Moderato — moderately

Allegro — at a quick pace, lively
Presto — very fast

DYNAMICS is a term meaning the degrees of intensity or volume of sound, which is varied to make the music more expressive.

Some of the generally used dynamic markings are listed here.

**p** (piano) soft
**mp** (mezzo piano) moderately soft

**mf** (mezzo forte) moderately loud
**f** (forte) loud

## THEMES FROM FAMOUS COMPOSITIONS

Play these excerpts in the correct tempos and with the appropriate dynamics.

A. Symphony No. 5 (last movement) — Ludwig van Beethoven (1770–1827)

B. Symphony No. 5 (first movement) — Peter Ilyich Tchaikovsky (1840–1893)

C. Symphony No. 1 (last movement) — Johannes Brahms (1833–1897)

D. Fugue in g minor (for organ) — Johann Sebastian Bach (1685–1750)

E. Symphony No. 104 (first movement) — Joseph Haydn (1732–1809)

67. THE ECHO

*Since Bach did not edit his music, there is no indication of tempo or dynamics. This fugue subject would suggest a moderato or an allegro tempo because of the vigorous character of the motive.

# Unit II
## EXERCISES FOR SCALE PREPARATION

Scale playing will require playing eight notes in succession (three
additional notes added to the five finger positions already learned).
Therefore the problem at the piano is: either turning the thumb
under a finger, or crossing a finger over the thumb.

Practice all three exercises first HANDS SEPARATELY, then
combine both hands. Turn the thumb under (or cross over one
of the other fingers) as smoothly as possible so there is an even,
legato sound.

(i)

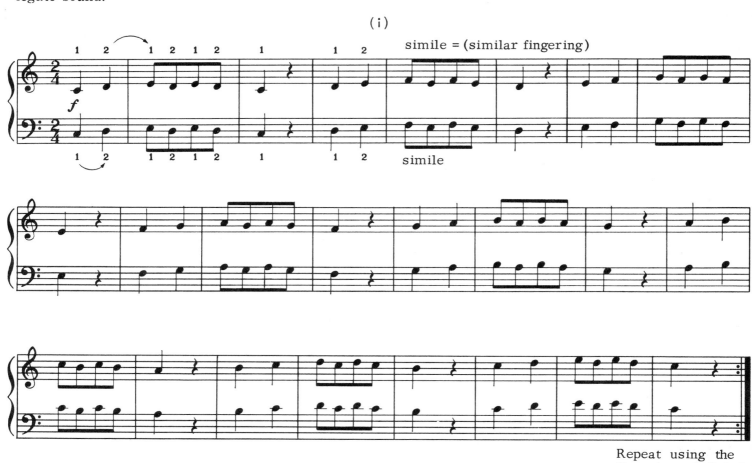

Repeat using the
fingerings: 1-3, 1-4.

(ii)

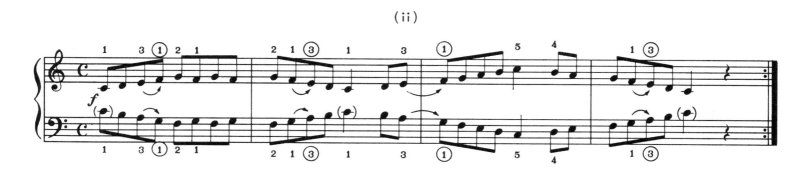

(iii)

## MAJOR SCALES

The MAJOR SCALE (from the word meaning ladder) uses seven different letters of the musical alphabet. However, because the scale begins and ends on the same letter, there are actually EIGHT tones altogether. These tones always appear in a regular pattern of whole steps and half steps.

## THE PATTERN FOR ALL MAJOR SCALES

EXAMPLE: C Major

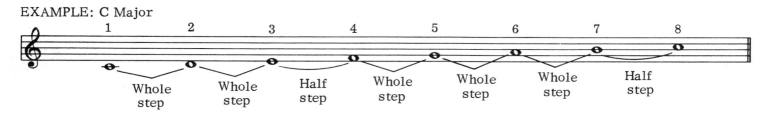

## THE FINGERING FOR MAJOR SCALES BEGINNING ON WHITE KEYS

The fingering is the *same* for the scales of C, G, D, A and E Major. Because of the arrangement of black keys on the piano, the scales of F and B Major use slightly different fingerings.

Play the C Major Scale (given in the example below) both ascending and descending (read the finger numbers backwards for descending), first with the Right Hand, then with the Left Hand. *Memorize* this fingering pattern.

Write the notes and fingerings for the scales of G, D, A and E in the space provided; then play these in order. Notice the *change* of fingering in the B Scale (Left Hand), and in the F Scale (Right Hand).

EXAMPLE:

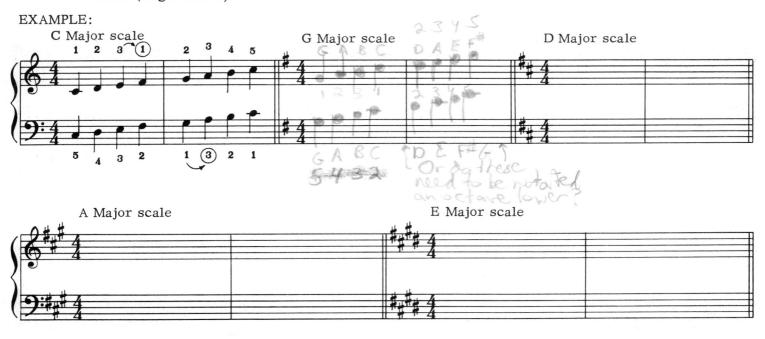

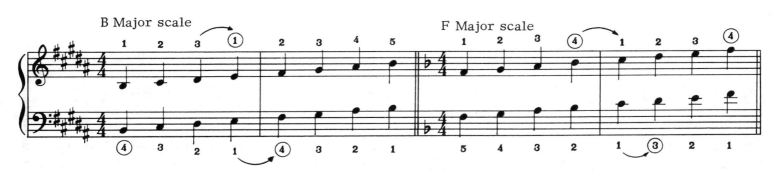

Play *The First Noel* **HANDS SEPARATELY** at first, then combine both hands. Think ahead for turning the thumb under in
the R.H., or crossing 3 over 1 in the L.H.

Transpose this song to other keys (scales).

68. THE FIRST NOEL

French Carol

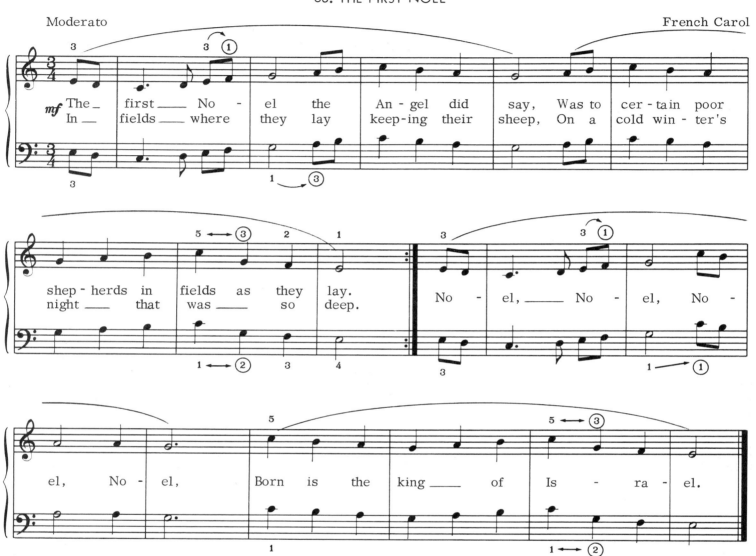

Moderato

The _ first ____ No - el the An - gel did say, Was to a cer - tain poor
In _ fields ____ where they lay keep-ing their sheep, On a cold win - ter's

shep - herds in fields as they lay.
night ____ that was ____ so deep.

No - el, ____ No - el, No -

el, No - el, Born is the king ____ of Is - ra - el.

Transpose this song to other keys (scales).

EXAMPLES:

# Unit 11
## EXERCISE FOR REPEATED NOTES

Practice this exercise before playing *Away in a Manger* to acquire
facility in changing fingers.

An interval of a SEVENTH is a large skip requiring an extended
position between the thumb and 5th finger (either space, space;
or line, line).

EXAMPLES:

### 69. AWAY IN A MANGER

Mark the changes in hand positions.

# Unit 11

RITARDANDO (rit.) indicates a change in tempo and means to slow down gradually. A TEMPO means to resume the original tempo (the basic speed of the composition).

## 70. DISTANT LAND

Observe the dynamics in the composition below. Mark the changes in hand positions.

Other DYNAMIC MARKINGS:

Crescendo (cresc.) means to grow louder and is often represented by the sign: ———◁

Decrescendo (decresc.) means to grow softer and is often represented by the sign: ▷———

Greensleeves is a famous old English tune dating back to the 16th century. Since then it has been heard in many different versions, one of the most beautiful is an arrangement for orchestra by the Twentieth Century composer, Ralph Vaughn Williams (1872-1958).

Notice that in the arrangement on this page there is a minor ending in the 15th measure, and a Major ending in the 31st measure.

## 71. GREENSLEEVES

Observe the dynamics. Mark the changes in hand positions.

SYNCOPATION (or SYNCOPATED RHYTHM) is a rhythmic effect of placing accents on normally weak beats. This may be accomplished in several ways.

EXAMPLES:

1. A longer note on a weak beat:

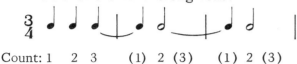

Count: 1 2 (3) 4     1 2 (3) 4

2. A rest on a strong beat:

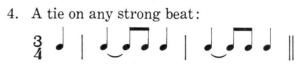

Count: (1) 2 (3) 4     (1) 2 (3) 4

3. A tie over the first strong beat:

Count: 1 2 3    (1) 2 (3)    (1) 2 (3)

4. A tie on any strong beat:

Count: 3   1 (2) & 3   1 (2) & 3

An interval of an OCTAVE is a large skip requiring an extended position between the thumb and 5th fingers (either line, space; or space, line).

EXAMPLES:

## SIGHT READING STUDIES EMPHASIZING SHIFTING HAND POSITIONS

### 72. WALTZ

Each change of hand position will be indicated by a circled finger number.

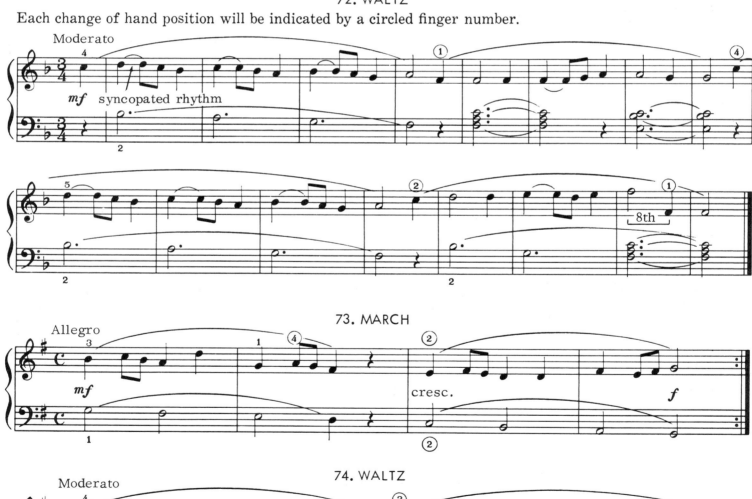

### 73. MARCH

### 74. WALTZ

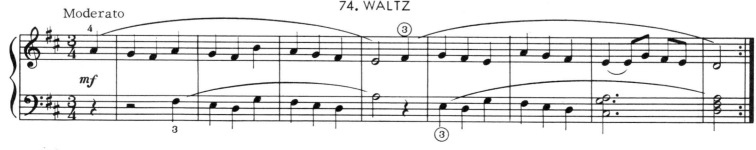

FIRST and SECOND ENDINGS: Play the first eight measures
of the *Etude* below. Repeat back to the beginning from the repeat
sign in the eighth measure (1st ending). When playing through
for the second time, omit the 1st ending and play the last two
measures (2nd ending).

## 75. ETUDE

## SCALES IN CONTRARY MOTION (optional)

Play the scales below in contrary motion, first the R.H., then the
L.H., then combine both hands. Also play the scales of G, A, and
E Major in the same manner.

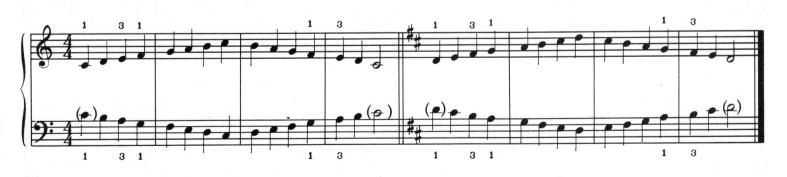

# Unit 11

76. AMERICAN PATROL
Duet
Secondo

F. W. Meacham
Arr. by J. W. B.

## 76. AMERICAN PATROL
### Duet
### Primo

F. W. Meacham
Arr. by J. W. B.

## REVIEW QUIZ No. 5

I.  Write in the missing letters which spell V7 chords, and name the key to which it be-
    longs.  (A half step above the first letter of the chord is the key note.)
    EXAMPLE:

    1. __E__ Bb __C__ V7 chord in __F__        5. D ____ ____ V7 chord in ____
    2. ____ ____ A V7 chord in ____            6. ____ Eb ____ V7 chord in ____
    3. ____ F ____ V7 chord in ____            7. C ____ ____ V7 chord in ____
    4. G♯ ____ ____ V7 chord in ____           8. ____ C ____ V7 chord in ____

II. Answer the following questions.
    EXAMPLE:
    1. The rhythm ♩ ♫ may be counted __1 & da__ .
    2. The names of the portions of three part song form are _____ _____ _____ .
    3. The degree of intensity or volume of sound in music is called _____ .
    4. Half steps occur in Major scales between _____ and _____ .
    5. The B Major scale has a different fingering in the _____ and F Major
       in the _____ .
    6. Syncopated rhythm is _____ .

III. Give the abbreviations for the following musical terms, and tell what they mean.
     EXAMPLE:
     1. Piano __p__ ; and means __soft__
     2. Mezzo piano ____ ; and means _____ _____
     3. Forte ____ ; and means _____
     4. Mezzo forte ____ ; and means _____ _____
     5. Ritardando ____ ; and means _____
     6. Crescendo ____ ; and means _____
     7. Decrescendo ____ ; and means _____

IV. Draw a note above the one given to form the following intervals.

EXAMPLE:

5th    4th    2nd    8th    7th    3rd    6th    7th    2nd    3rd    4th    7th

V.  Play the chord progression I, IV, I, V7, I in all keys without looking at the keyboard
    for the chord changes.

GP23

# Unit 12

- Legato and staccato touch combined
- The chromatic scale
- Broken-chord basses
- The subdominant chord in minor
- Root position chords
- Strumming accompaniments
- Duets
- Review quiz No. 6

## VARIETIES OF TOUCH

LEGATO and STACCATO are the two basic types of touch on the piano, and it is possible to combine these (legato in one hand and staccato in the other). Practice the exercises below for touch control.

Transpose chromatically upward to all other keys.

(i) LEGATO             (ii) STACCATO             (iii) LEGATO AND STACCATO

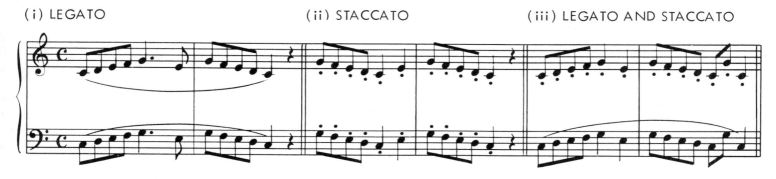

Practice using the touches suggested above.        Practice using the touches suggested above.
Transpose chromatically upward to all other keys.        Transpose — keys of G, F, D, A

(iv)                                                    (v)

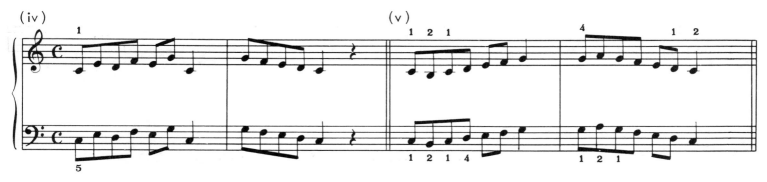

# Unit 12

## LEGATO and STACCATO COMBINED

### 77. MARCH I

Daniel Gottlieb Türk
(1756-1813)

### 78. MARCH II

Türk

### 79. ROW, ROW, ROW YOUR BOAT

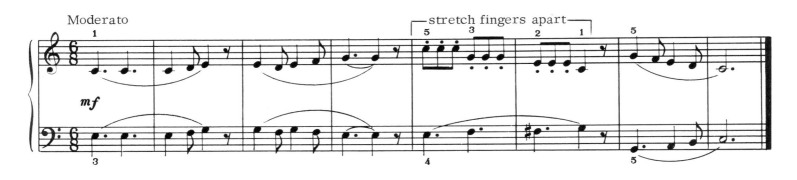

### 80. TOUCH STUDY

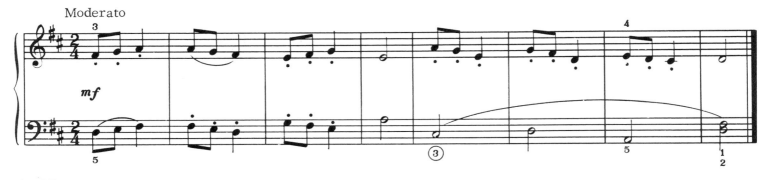

## THE CHROMATIC SCALE

The CHROMATIC SCALE either ascends or descends by half steps. The standard fingering for this scale is: 3 on all the black keys, the thumb on *single* white keys, and 1-2 on *adjoining* white keys (E-F and B-C).

Practice the drill below to attain facility with the chromatic scale fingering pattern. Play first HANDS SEPARATELY, then together. Practice three tempos: slow, medium, fast.

Continue the chromatic scale upward in the same manner. Add one higher note each time until the range is an entire octave (from C to C).

### 81. ETUDE IN D MINOR

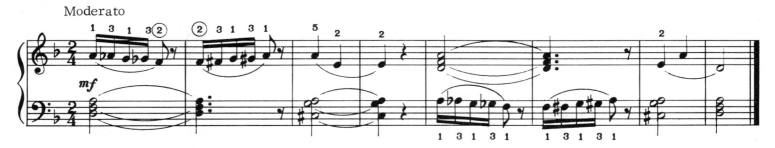

### *A CHROMATIC MELODY

*Fugue motive from Bach's *Chromatic Fantasy and Fugue*

# Unit 12
## BROKEN-CHORD HARMONIZING

Harmonization has been limited so far to primarily the "block" chord accompaniment (all tones played simultaneously). In the "broken" chord accompaniment the tones are separated in the various ways shown below.

Practice the harmonic progression above in ALL KEYS, first H.S.,* then together. Do not look at the keyboard for the change of chords.

A slight change in the position of the V7 chord is frequently used in broken-chord harmonizing: Practice this slight change as a substitute for the V7 chord in the pattern above.

Any change in hand position is indicated by a circled finger number.

### 82. GERMAN FOLK SONG

* H.S. – Hands separately

TROUBLE SPOTS: Within each composition there are usually
a few measures that cause difficulty. However if these measures
are practiced as preparatory exercises, before actually playing
the composition, the difficulties will diminish.

Practice the two preparatory exercises below observing the difficulties indicated.

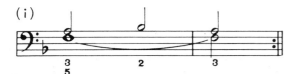

(i)

Holding 5 while playing 3-2-3.

(ii)

Changing quickly from 1 to 5-4.

## 83. AULD LANG SYNE

Scotch Air
Words, Robert Burns

# Unit 12

Play *My Bonnie* as written then repeat using the other type of broken-chord waltz bass.

EXAMPLE:

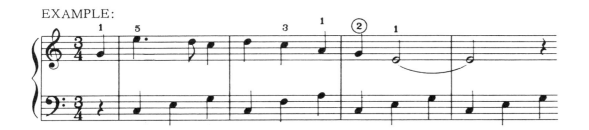

### 84. MY BONNIE

College Song

Moderato

My Bon - nie lies o-ver the o-cean,___ My Bon - nie lies o-ver the sea.___

___ My Bon - nie lies o-ver the o-cean,___ Oh, bring back My Bon - nie to me.___

(Chorus)

Bring back, bring back, Oh, bring back My Bon - nie to me, to

me, Bring back, bring back, Oh, bring back My Bon - nie to me.___

As a preparatory exercise practice the slurred notes below saying
the words "down-up" for the changes in wrist position.

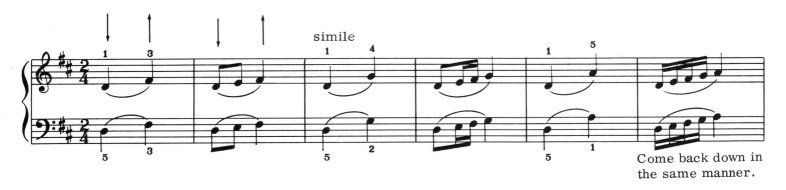

## 85. POLLY WOLLY DOODLE

American Folk Song

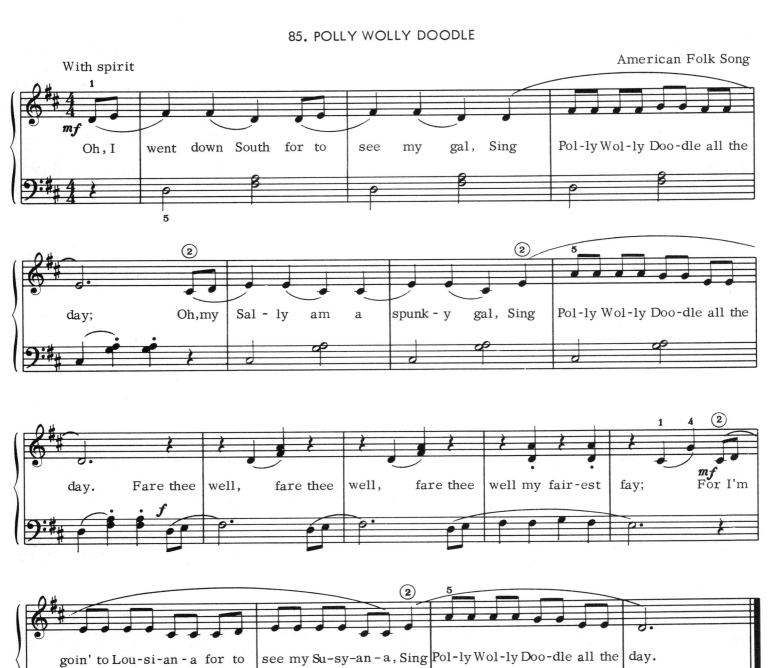

# Unit 12

REVIEW OF SIGHT READING PROCEDURE:

Notice: 1. Key and time signature
   2. Tempo
   3. Shift in hand position (as indicated by circled finger numbers)
   4. Legato and staccato
   5. Dynamics

## 86. THE MARINES' HYMN

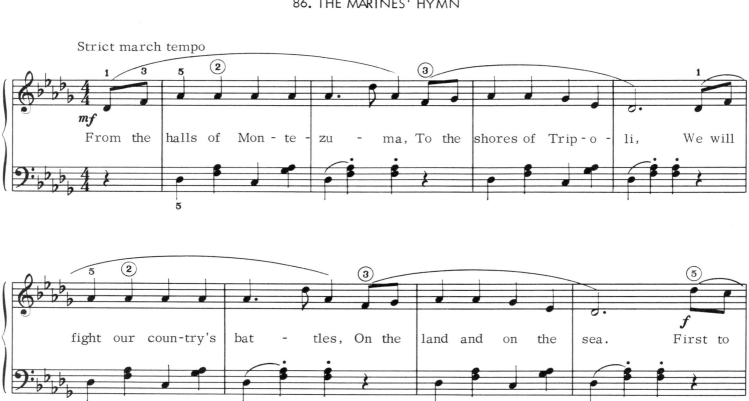

From the halls of Mon-te-zu - ma, To the shores of Trip-o-li, We will

fight our coun-try's bat - tles, On the land and on the sea. First to

fight for right and free - dom, And to keep our hon-or clean, We are

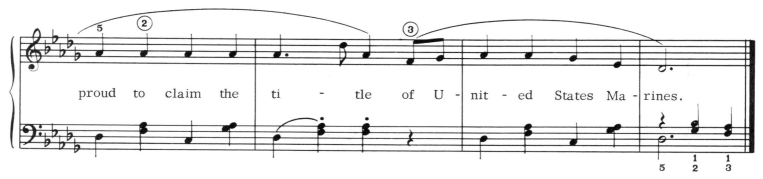

proud to claim the ti - tle of U - nit - ed States Ma - rines.

# Unit 12
## THE SUBDOMINANT CHORD (iv Chord) IN MINOR

To form a iv chord in minor begin with a minor chord position,
then follow the rules below.

| LEFT HAND | RIGHT HAND |
|---|---|
| 1. Keep the 5th finger the same. | 1. Keep 1 the same. |
| 2. Play 2 (in the five finger position). | 2. Move 3 up a whole step. |
| 3. Move 1 up a half step. | 3. Move 5 up a half step. |

EXAMPLE:

EXAMPLE:

Practice the above pattern for all keys, first with L.H., then with
the R.H., then hands together. Also play the progression, i, iv, i,
V7, i in minor in the same manner. Do not look at the keyboard
for the chord changes.

ACCELERANDO (accel.) means to increase in speed gradually.
This is a typical effect in gypsy music.

### 87. DARK EYES

# Unit 12
## CHORDS IN ROOT POSITION

All chords are referred to by their ROOT NAME. This name is derived from the scale to which the chords belong. Each degree of the scale is given a name, either Roman numerals (I, IV, V), or scale degree names (tonic, subdominant, dominant), or letter names (C chord, F chord, G chord). These chords (I, IV, V) are called PRIMARY CHORDS because they are the most frequently used chords.

EXAMPLE:

SCALE DEGREE NUMBERS 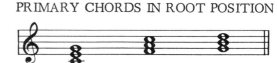 PRIMARY CHORDS IN ROOT POSITION

Chords I and IV are three-tone chords (triads). These are constructed by intervals of thirds above the root (root, third, fifth). The V7 chord is a four-tone chord and is also constructed by intervals of thirds above the root (root, third, fifth, seventh).

Only the I chord has been used in root position so far. Chords IV and V7 have been used in inverted (rearranged) position for easy playing.

EXAMPLES:

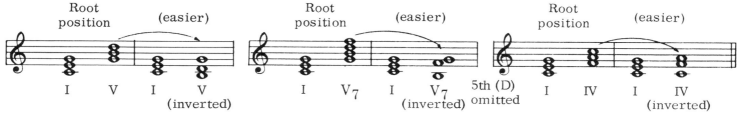

### CHORD DRILLS

Play the following chord patterns. Transpose to other keys. Do not look at the keyboard for chord changes.

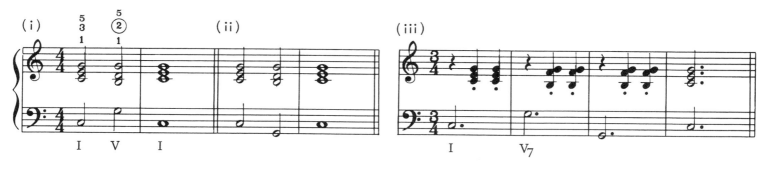

# Unit 12

## CHORDING OR STRUMMING ACCOMPANIMENT

The chord patterns at the bottom of the previous page were designed as an introduction to STRUMMING an accompaniment. This is the style used when someone else is singing or playing a tune.

Sing the melody and chord the accompaniment for *Polly Wolly Doodle* in the following manner. (Another person may play the melody an octave higher as a duet.)

EXAMPLE:

Sing the melody and chord the accompaniment to *My Bonnie* in the following manner.

EXAMPLE:

Write in the appropriate chords in strumming fashion to *The Marines' Hymn*. Then play the entire accompaniment in the same manner while singing the melody.

# Unit 12

## 88. DUET
### Secondo

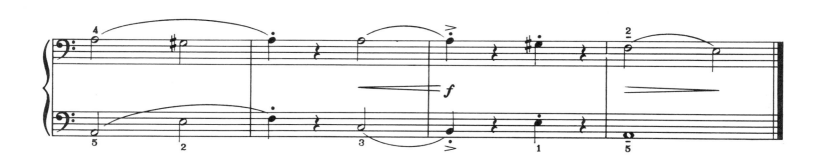

## 89. DUET
### Secondo

## 88. DUET
Primo

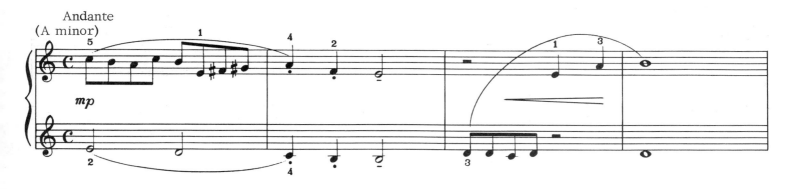

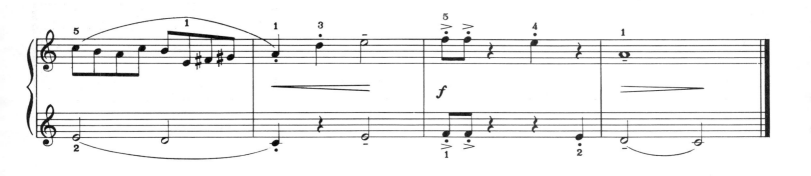

## 89. DUET
Primo

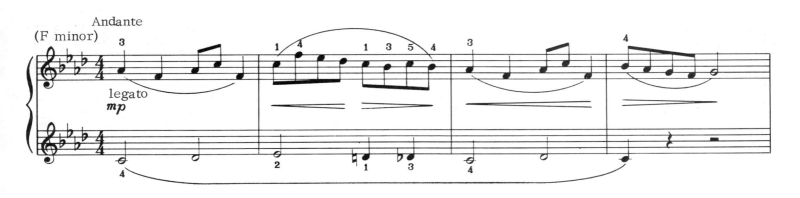

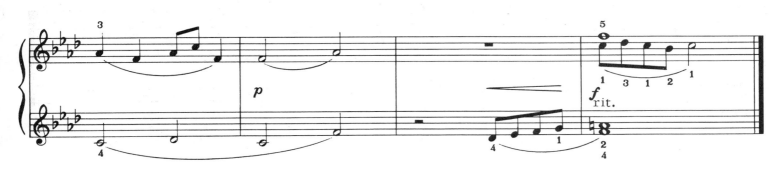

# Unit 12
## REVIEW QUIZ NO. 6

I. Write key signatures in the following Major keys. (In sharp
keys think up an alphabet letter from the last sharp; In flat
keys think second to the last flat with exception of F and C.)

EXAMPLE:

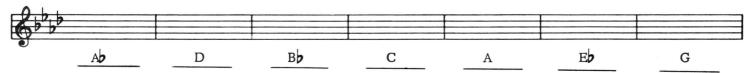

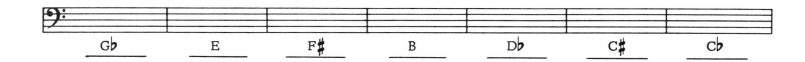

II. Write the scales of D and E Major without key signatures.
Place the sharps before the notes to be affected. Also write
the correct fingering.

III. Write a waltz bass accompaniment that corresponds to the
Roman numerals on the staff below.

EXAMPLE:

IV. Write a broken-chord bass that corresponds to the Roman
numerals on the staff below.

EXAMPLE:

V. Write dominant seventh chords in root position in the key of
the tonic chord given.

EXAMPLE:

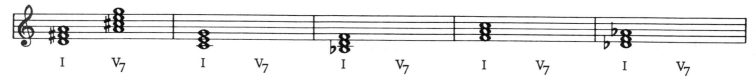

GP23

# Unit 13

- Major scales, beginning on black keys
- The damper pedal and pedal studies
- The extended broken-chord accompaniment
- The V-7 chord in root position
- Duets
- Review quiz No. 7

## THE FINGERING FOR MAJOR SCALES
## BEGINNING ON BLACK KEYS

The scales of B♭, E♭, A♭, D♭ and G♭ Major all begin on black keys.
The fingering for these five scales is similar. The FIRST WHITE
KEY after a black key in the RIGHT HAND ASCENDING uses
the THUMB. The first WHITE KEY after a black key in the
LEFT HAND DESCENDING uses the THUMB.

RIGHT HAND ASCENDING

LEFT HAND DESCENDING

EXAMPLE: B♭ Major Scale

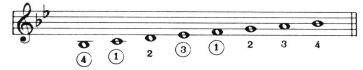

Practice the five scales on this page first hands separately, then
together.

E♭ MAJOR SCALE

A♭ MAJOR SCALE

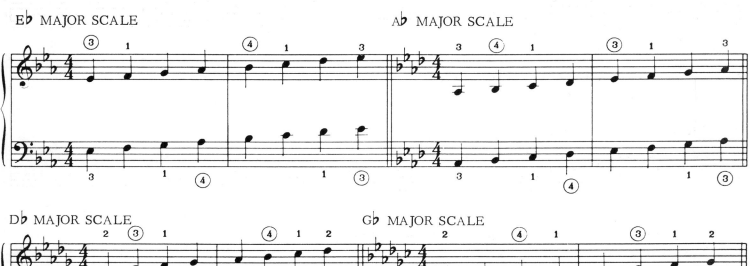

D♭ MAJOR SCALE

G♭ MAJOR SCALE

# Unit 13

## VARIETY IN ACCOMPANIMENTS

The song *Fais Do Do* below is harmonized with a broken-chord accompaniment. It would be advisable to first practice this composition with block chords.

This song could also be harmonized with a "waltz" style bass. Observe the dynamics, and listen carefully for the correct BALANCE between melody and harmony.

### 90. FAIS DO DO
(Go to Sleep)

French Folk Song

## HARMONIC ANALYSIS

For a thorough understanding of chords and chordal positions, it is advisable to mentally "play" through each composition before actually playing it at the piano.

Notice the chord positions outlined in the right hand melody line in the song below.

EXAMPLE:

Measures 1 - 2    3 - 4    5    6    7    8

### 91. GERMAN FOLK SONG

Write in the correct finger numbers.

Notice the movement of the right and left hands at intervals of 6ths and octaves in the song below.

### 92. AU CLAIR DE LA LUNE

Write in the correct finger numbers.

French Folk Song

Au clair de la lu - ne, Mon a - mi Pier - rot, Prê - te moi ta plu - me Pour é - crire un mot;

Ma chan - delle est mor - te, Je n'ai plus de feu. Ou - vre moi ta por - te, Pour l'a mour de Dieu.

# Unit 13

Practice the exercise below to increase the speed of playing. Begin
very slowly, then play faster, and finally as fast as possible. Also
play with varieties of touches: legato; staccato; legato and staccato combined; one hand louder than the other for balance.

Transpose to all other keys.

EXERCISE FOR FINGER DEXTERITY

The DAMPER PEDAL (on the right) releases the dampers from the strings and allows the strings to vibrate freely. This pedal is generally used to bind together similar harmonies between the treble and bass, in a sonorous manner.

Place the heel solidly on the floor and push and release the pedal according to the sign:

down                     up

Be sure not to blur the harmonies when using the damper pedal.

## PEDAL STUDIES

# Unit 13

## THE EXTENDED BROKEN-CHORD ACCOMPANIMENT

Practice the drill below which will enable you to provide more interesting accompaniments. This type of extended broken-chord bass is the typical "oom-pah-pah" accompaniment suitable for waltzes.

Notice the change in fingering for the tonic chord (beginning on 4 instead of 5). Think ahead for the extension between the tonic and dominant notes.

Transpose to all other keys.

### 93. BLOW THE MAN DOWN

Circle the Right Hand finger numbers to indicate changes in hand positions.

Old Sea Chantey

# Unit 13
## THE V-7 CHORD IN ROOT POSITION

A solid bass effect is established when the root of the dominant
seventh chord is played first, rather than playing the third of the
chord first in inverted position.

EXAMPLES:

ROOT IN BASS → 7th, 5th omitted, 3rd, Root    Played    THIRD IN BASS → Root, 7th, 5th omitted, 3rd    Played

Practice the chord progression below in all keys until the changes
are automatic.  Notice the change in fingering for the tonic chord.

### 94. LA TRAVIATA
Parigi o cara
from Act III

Circle the Right Hand finger numbers to indicate changes in hand
positions.

Giuseppe Verdi
(1813–1901)
Arr. by J.W.B.

Andante

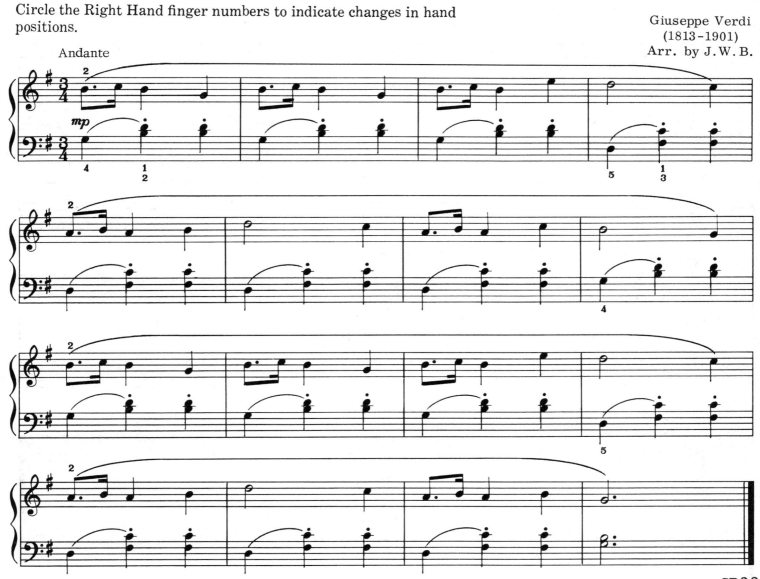

# Unit 13

CHORDAL DISTRIBUTION is often necessary for a better acoustical effect. The notes within chords will be distributed between the two hands to avoid overemphasizing and doubling certain tones. Ordinarily the 3rd of the chord will not be doubled (as in measure 2) especially when this note appears in the melody.

## 95. WHEN JOHNNY COMES MARCHING HOME

Circle the Right Hand finger numbers to indicate changes in hand positions.

Strict march tempo
(G minor)

Louis Lambert

When John - ny Comes March - ing Home a - gain, Hur - rah,____ hur - rah!____ We'll give him a heart - y wel - come then. Hur - rah,____ hur - rah!____ The____ men will cheer and the boys will shout, The la - dies they__will all turn out, And we'll

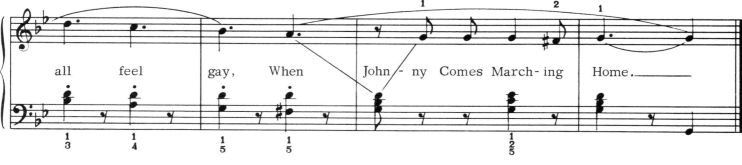

all feel gay, When John - ny Comes March - ing Home.____

*Country Gardens* has all of the various problems in hand positions discussed so far: finger extension, contraction, repeated notes, the shift of hand position. Therefore circle the finger numbers to indicate these various changes (as in measure 2), and label the type of change.

Be careful with the dotted rhythms: Within each quarter beat there are four sixteenth notes, so the dotted eighth and sixteenth may be counted by saying "1, 2, 3, 4" very quickly:

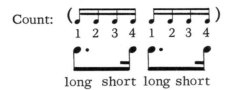

## 96. COUNTRY GARDENS

English Folk Dance

# Unit 13

## 97. DUET
### Secondo

Andante con moto

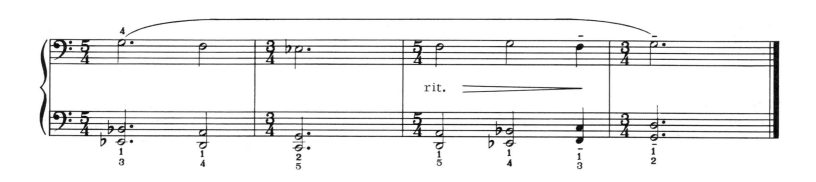

## 98. DUET
### Secondo

Allegro

# Unit 13

## 97. DUET
### Primo

Andante con moto

## 98. DUET
### Primo

Allegro

# Unit 13
## REVIEW QUIZ NO. 7

I. Write the scales of B♭ and E♭ Major without key signatures. Place the flats before the notes to be affected. Also write the correct fingering.

II. Write the following pattern in the keys indicated; then play these.

EXAMPLE:

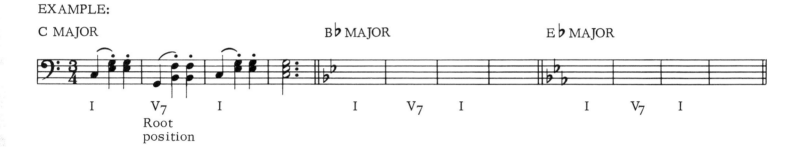

III. Write key signatures in the following Major keys.

EXAMPLE:

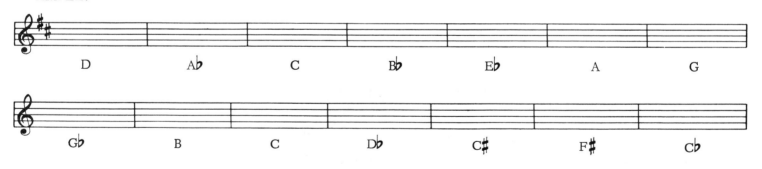

IV. Write a broken-chord bass that corresponds to the Roman numerals on the staff below.

EXAMPLE:
E minor

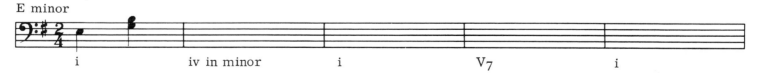

V. Write the chromatic scale ascending and descending.

EXAMPLE:

GP23

# SECTION THREE

# FUNCTIONAL PIANO

PIANOFORTE (18th Century)
Photo courtesy of the Metropolitan Museum of Art. Crosby
Brown Collection of Musical Instruments. This instrument was
built in 1720 by Bartolomeo Cristofori, inventor of the piano-
forte. The instrument pictured here may be seen in the New
York Metropolitan Museum of Art. It is one of the two existing
Cristofori pianos.

# SECTION THREE

## FUNCTIONAL PIANO

*Functional piano* is a term meaning the ability to operate (or function) at the keyboard — thus, to be able to improvise. The material presented thus far has been designed to give the student the necessary background for improvisation (chord knowledge, finger exercises, accompaniment styles, etc.). SECTION THREE was incorporated into the text as a whole because of the frequent usage, application, and demands made of musicians in general in this important area.

Reading music quickly and efficiently is often necessary for practical applications — such is the case for the general classroom teacher in the elementary school. He is often called upon to accompany students at the piano while they sing from their song books. These books usually have only single line melodies and sometimes chord symbols but do not indicate the piano accompaniment. It is therefore up to the teacher to improvise a suitable accompaniment that will be appropriate for the style and character of the song (march, waltz, folk song, etc.).

Another field that demands "on the spot" improvised accompaniments is music therapy. The therapist must be able to function effectively at the piano for numerous duties demanded of him in his profession.

Any music educator would also be expected to be a "functional pianist" being able to play simple accompaniments whenever the occasion might arise. Pianists are even frequently asked to accompany without music.

The skills established in SECTION THREE are:
1. improvising from chord symbols
2. improvising accompaniments to single line melodies harmonized with two chords
3. improvising accompaniments to single line melodies harmonized with three chords.
4. improvising accompaniments to single line melodies harmonized with secondary chords
5. improvising accompaniments to single line melodies that modulate (four or more chords)

Review the accompaniment styles learned in the previous units for help in choosing effective accompaniments to the following melodies presented in Units 14 and 15.

# UNIT 14

- Chord symbols
- Melodies to be harmonized with two chords (I, V7)
- Melodies to be harmonized with three chords (I, IV, V7)
- Review quiz No. 8

## CHANGE IN TERMINOLOGY FOR CHORDS

The traditional method of indicating chords either by Roman numerals or by scale degree names (tonic, subdominant, dominant, etc.) is necessary for formal analysis. However for harmonization of simple melodies such as folk music, marches, dances, and popular music, this method is somewhat cumbersome and slow when applied to functional improvisation. Therefore a more contemporary system of chord symbolization has evolved which is simple, direct, and fast in application. This method of chord symbolization is expressed by *letter names* only, such as, C, Gm, G7, etc.

Single line melodies (frequently called "lead sheets") indicate only melody (either with or without words) and letter-name chord symbols. The lead sheet is a product of music in the entertainment field, but also carries over into music education. Some of the newer song books in the schools are now being notated in this manner.

### CHORD SYMBOLS

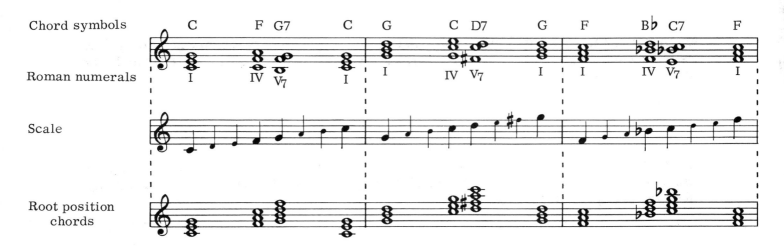

Play the rhythm patterns below using chords indicated by the chord symbols. Practice first with the L.H., then the R.H., and finally, play both hands together.

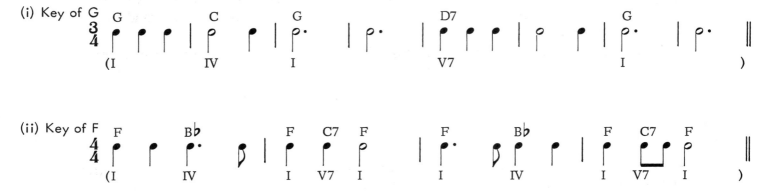

# Unit 14

## MELODIES TO BE HARMONIZED WITH TWO CHORDS

PRACTICE PROCEDURE

1. Recognize the key and play I-V7-I-V7-I as a preliminary drill.
2. Play a chord at the beginning of every measure even though it may be a repetition of the same chord.
3. First play the melody in the Right Hand and the chords in the Left. Repeat and play the melody in the Left Hand and the chords in the Right.
4. First use block chords only, then repeat using any of the broken chord patterns learned so far (pp. 86, 102, 103).
5. Do not look at the keyboard for the chord changes.

NON-CHORD TONES are those notes in the melody which do not fit into the chord played with them. These are momentary dissonances which will resolve on the next beat. Non-chord tones will be indicated by the sign: +

### 1. LONDON BRIDGE

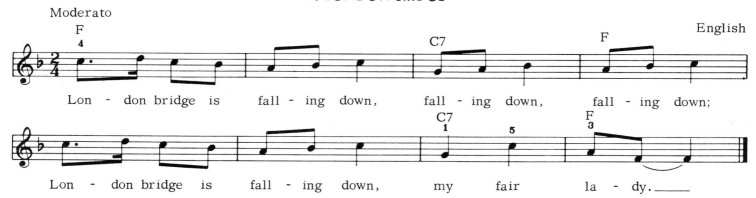

### 2. SKIP TO MY LOU

### 3. OH, DEAR, WHAT CAN THE MATTER BE?

# Unit 14

## 4. LONG, LONG AGO

Thomas H. Bayly

Tell me the tales that to me were so dear, Long, long a - go, Long, long a - go.

Sing me the songs I de - light - ed to hear, Long, long a - go, long a - go.

## 5. CLEMENTINE

American

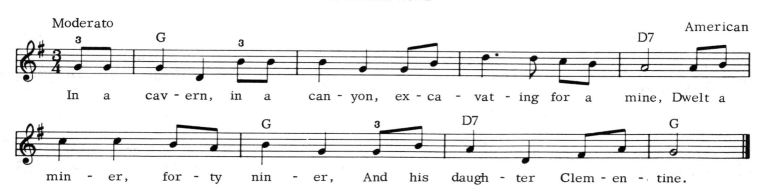

In a cav - ern, in a can - yon, ex - ca - vat - ing for a mine, Dwelt a

min - er, for - ty nin - er, And his daugh - ter Clem - en - tine.

## 6. SHOO, FLY, DON'T BOTHER ME!

American

Shoo, fly, don't both - er me! Shoo, fly, don't both - er me!

Shoo, fly, don't both - er me, 'cause I be - long to Comp - 'ny G!

## 7. FOLK SONG

French

GP23

# Unit 14

## MELODIES TO BE HARMONIZED WITH THREE CHORDS

Play I-IV-I-V7-I in the key of each piece before playing the melody and harmony together.

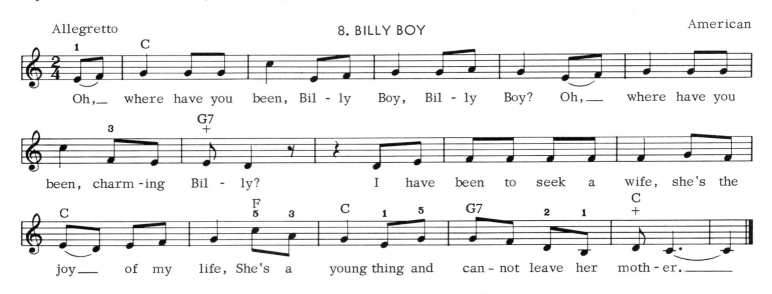

8. BILLY BOY — American

A GRACE NOTE is an added ornament to a main note or an ornamental figure between two notes. Grace notes do not receive any extra time value and are played quickly.

EXAMPLES:

9. LULLABY — Johannes Brahms (1833-1897)

10. GOOD-NIGHT, LADIES — College Song

Good - night, la - dies! Good - night, la - dies! Good - night, la - dies! We're

going to leave you now. Mer - ri -ly we roll a - long, Roll a - long, roll a - long,

Mer - ri - ly we roll a - long O - ver the dark blue sea.

# Unit 14

## 11. RED RIVER VALLEY

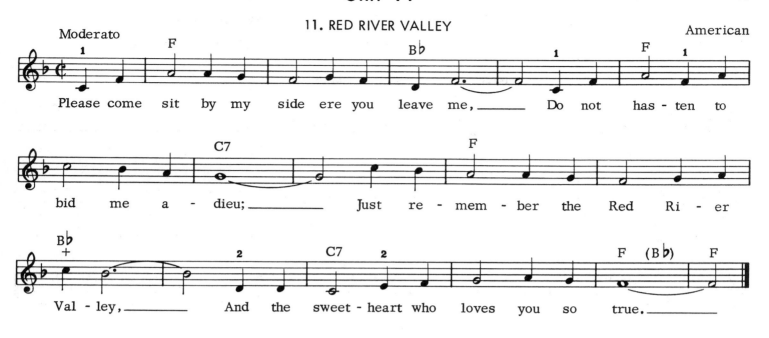

Please come sit by my side ere you leave me, _____ Do not has-ten to bid me a - dieu; _____ Just re - mem - ber the Red Ri - er Val - ley, _____ And the sweet-heart who loves you so true. _____

## 12. ON TOP OF OLD SMOKY

On top of old Smok - y, _____ All cov - ered with snow, _____ I lost my true lov - er, _____ By a - court - in' too slow. _____

## 13. SILENT NIGHT

Si - lent night, Ho - ly night, All is calm, All is bright, Round yon Vir - gin Moth - er and Child! Ho - ly In - fant so ten - der and mild, Sleep in heav - en - ly peace, — Sleep — in heav - en - ly peace.

GP23

Notice the syncopation in these two songs.  In the second measure of *Old Folks at Home:*

Andante con moto
**14. OLD FOLKS AT HOME**
Stephen Foster
(1826-1864)

Way down up - on the Swa - nee Riv - er, far, far a - way,

There's where my Heart is turn - ing ev - er, There's where the old folks stay.

All the world is sad and drear - y, Ev - 'ry where I roam;

Oh! Lord - y, how my heart grows wea - ry, Far from the old folks at home.

Clap and count the syncopation in the second, third, and fourth measures:

With spirit
(D minor)
**15. JOSHUA FOUGHT THE BATTLE OF JERICHO**
American Spiritual
Gm (iv chord in minor)

Josh - ua fought the bat - tle of ___ Jer - i - cho, ___ Jer - i - cho, ___

Jer - i - cho, ___ Josh - ua fought the bat - tle of ___ Jer - i - cho, ___ And the

walls came tum - blin' down. You may talk a - bout your King of

Gid - e - on, You may talk a - bout your men of Saul, There's

none like good old Josh - ua, At the bat - tle of Jer - i - cho.

### 16. TWO GUITARS

Slavic

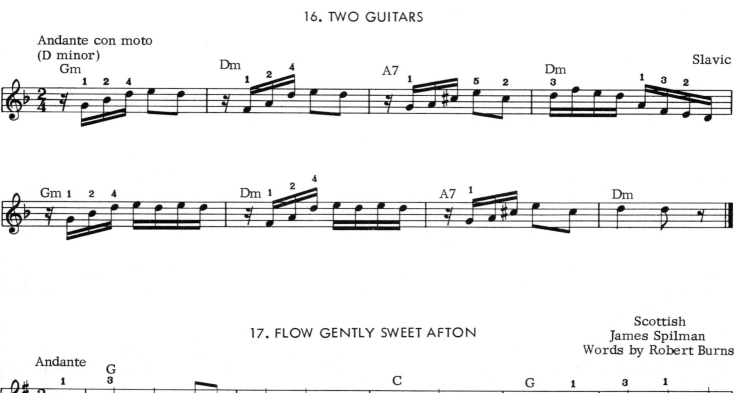

### 17. FLOW GENTLY SWEET AFTON

Scottish
James Spilman
Words by Robert Burns

Flow gen-tly, sweet Af-ton, A-mong thy green braes, flow gen-tly, I'll

sing thee a song in thy praise; My Mar-y's a-sleep by thy

mur-mur-ing stream, Flow gen-tly, sweet Af-ton, Dis-turb not her dream.

### 18. THE ARKANSAS TRAVELER

American

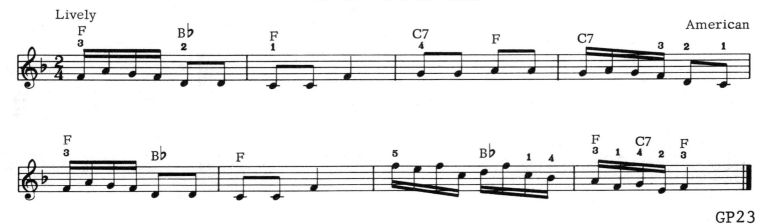

# Unit 14

## REVIEW QUIZ No. 8

I. Write the correct fingerings for the following Major scales, *away* from the keyboard.

**EXAMPLE:**

| D Major Scale | E♭ Major Scale | A♭ Major Scale |
|---|---|---|
| R.H. 1 2 3 1 2 3 4 5 | R.H. _____ | R.H. _____ |
| L.H. 5 4 3 2 1 3 2 1 | L.H. _____ | L.H. _____ |

II. Play the following broken chord drills. Transpose to minor.

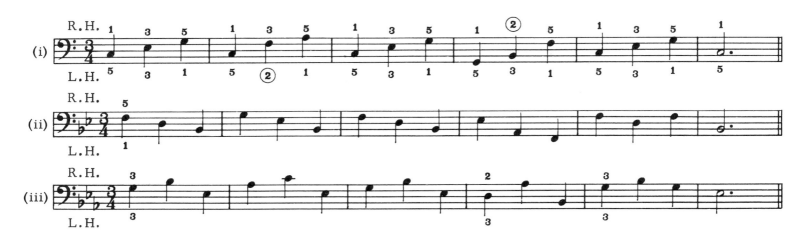

III. Write the correct harmony to the following melody. Use only two chords (I, V7). Play the melody and harmony together.

Austrian

EXAMPLE:   F   C7

IV. Write the correct harmony to the following melody. Use three chords (I, IV, V7). Play the melody and harmony together.

German

D

- Figured bass
- Inversions of chords
- A new chord progression (ii6 , I $\frac{6}{4}$ , V, I)
- Modulation (V7/V, V7/IV)
- Melodies to be harmonized with four or more chords
- Review quiz No. 9

## FIGURED BASS

Historically FIGURED BASS was a system of musical shorthand whereby chords were indicated by figures placed below the bass line. These figures indicate the exact position (inversion) of the chords, and in this respect the figured bass is more descriptive than chord symbolization. Present day usage of musical shorthand is left almost entirely to chord symbolization, but this system does not indicate the exact inversion of the chords. The improvisor must choose his own position of the chords from the indicated symbols.

Notice in the example below that the completion (realization) of the figured bass will result in three other parts (voices) added above the given bass. This is called four-part harmony: soprano, alto, tenor, bass.

The number 6 indicates first inversion chords in the figured bass and $\frac{6}{4}$ indicates second inversion chords. (Inversions will be explained on the next page.)

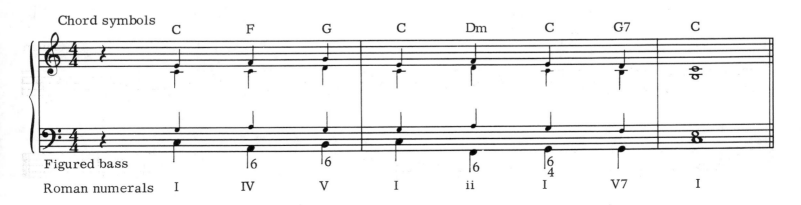

# Unit 15

## INVERSIONS OF CHORDS

A chord is inverted (rearranged) when any note other than the root is the lowest note of the chord. There are three possible positions for three-note chords: ROOT POSITION (root in the bass); FIRST INVERSION (3rd in the bass); SECOND INVERSION (5th in the bass). Four-note chords have either the root, 3rd, 5th, or 7th in the bass.

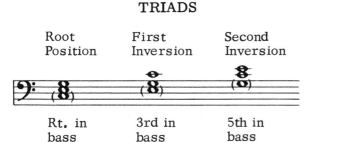

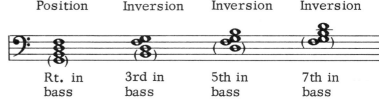

The figures (numbers) for the figured bass are derived from the intervals within the chords, and are measured from the bass note to the top note, and from the bass note to the middle note of the chord (for three-note chords). The principle is the same for four-note chords.

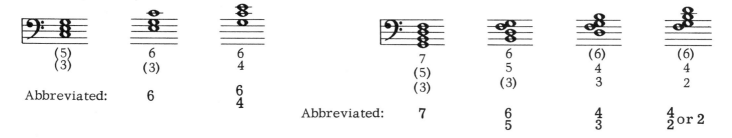

Practice the chord drill below for the correct fingerings of inversions. Transpose to all other keys.

## CHORD DRILL: INVERSIONS OF CHORDS

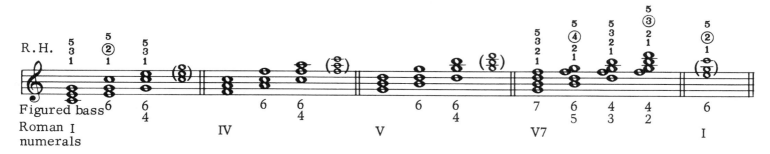

## I-V7-I PROGRESSION WITH INVERSIONS OF THE TONIC CHORD

It is important to be able to start on any position of the tonic chord and make the logical connections to the dominant seventh chord. Observe the smooth connection between chords in the following illustration.

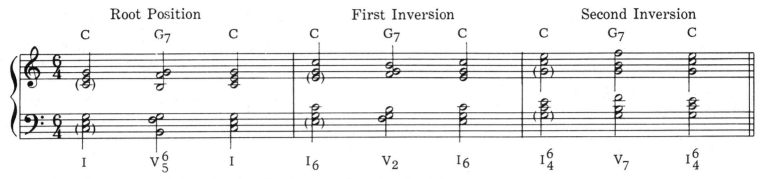

Practice the patterns below for facility in changing chords. Play the patterns ascending through the octave, first in the Major mode, then in minor. Observe the correct fingering. Do not look at the keyboard for chord changes.

Play with the Left Hand only. Start this chord drill in the key of G for the best keyboard register. Transpose chromatically upward.

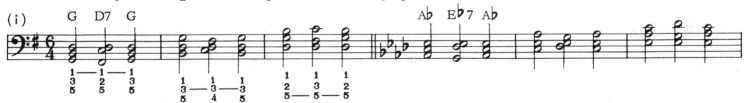

Play the chords in the Right Hand and roots in the Left Hand.

(OPTIONAL) Play first inversion chords ascending chromatically, then play second inversion chords ascending chromatically.

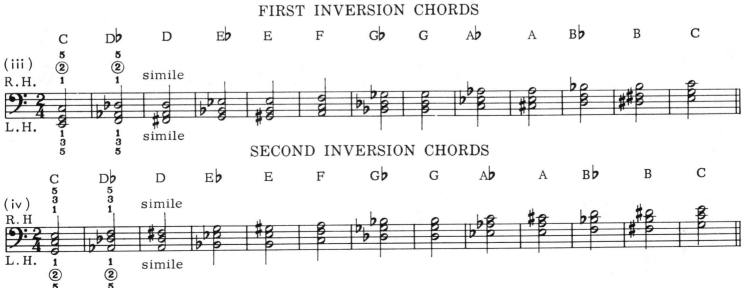

# Unit 15

## A NEW CHORD PROGRESSION

An often used chord progression is: I, ii6, I$_4^6$, V, I. This progression makes a very strong ending to a composition. After practicing this pattern in the chord drill below, use this progression in the *Battle Hymn of the Republic* (measures 7-8 and 15-16).

## CHORD DRILL: INTRODUCING THE ii CHORD (ii6)

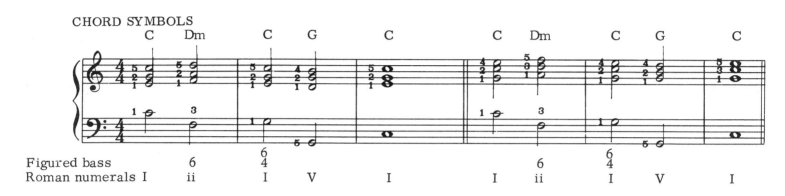

### 19. BATTLE HYMN OF THE REPUBLIC

William Steffe

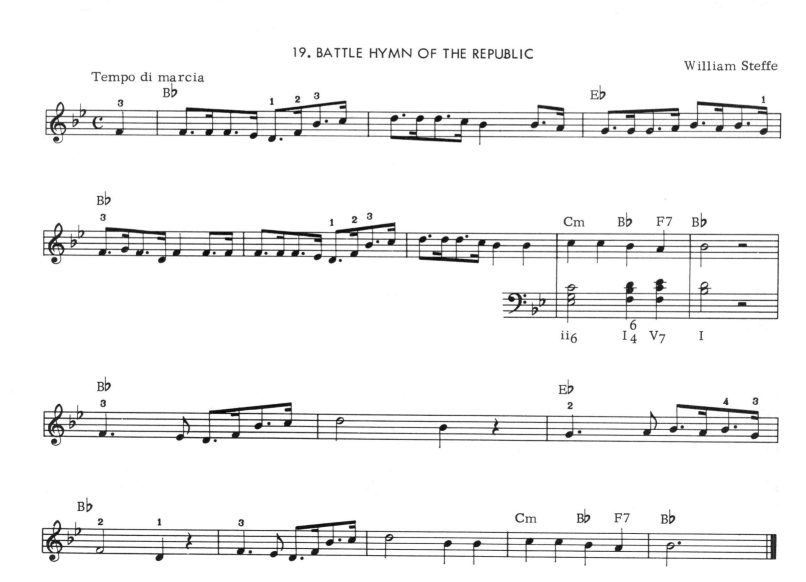

Play this chord progression in preparation for measures 5-6.

## 20. AMERICA

Henry Carey
Words by Samuel F. Smith

My coun - try 'tis of thee, Sweet land of lib - er - ty,
(ii6)                                                    (IV)

Of thee I sing. Land where my fa - thers died, Land of the
(ii6  I$^6_4$  V7  I)

Pil - grim's pride, From ev - 'ry__ moun - tain side Let__ free - dom ring.

## PATTERN DRILL: V7 TO I

Practice the pattern drill below in all keys for a frequently used
V7 to I progression. The Left Hand (5-2) fingering should be
legato.

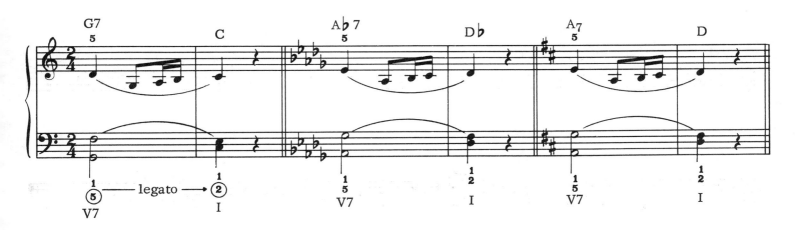

# Unit 15

## MODULATION

Harmonization has been limited so far to the three basic chords (I, IV, V) within the tonic key. However many songs require a shift to a new tonality momentarily, then a return to the main key. This shift, or abandoning of one tonality and establishing a new one, is called MODULATION.

Modulation is often affected by playing the dominant of the new key and resolving to the new key. Dominants such as these are called SECONDARY DOMINANTS.

The chord symbolization remains the same for the secondary dominants: D7, C7, etc. The Roman numerals, however, are frequently used in relation to the new key: V7 of V (modulation to the key of the dominant); V7 of IV (modulation to the key of the subdominant). Study the modulations below and play all the patterns. The secondary dominants will be marked with an X.

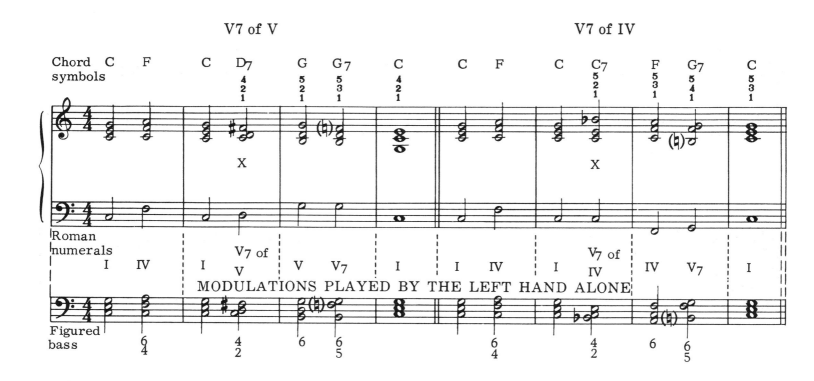

## V7/V CHORDS OF THE FREQUENTLY USED KEYS

Play the following chords, and think V7/V in the tonic key.

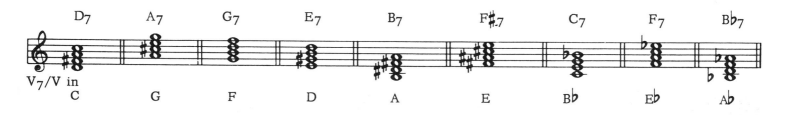

### V7/V CHORDS PLAYED BY THE LEFT HAND ALONE

$(V^4_2/V)$

## MELODIES TO BE HARMONIZED WITH FOUR OR MORE CHORDS

The melodies on the following pages are to be harmonized with the chords already learned (I, IV, V) plus the chord progression that incorporates the ii chord, and also secondary dominants. The first group of melodies do not modulate outside the tonic key, but they do incorporate the ii chord (occasionally the vi chord).

Harmonization of the following melodies becomes more involved with modulations either to the dominant or subdominant through the secondary dominants.

Play the song below (which is notated as an example) and notice the modulations to the dominant (measures 7-8), and to the subdominant (12-13).

### 21. WE GATHER TOGETHER

# Unit 15

The following melodies may be harmonized with chords in root position (for easy playing), or may be harmonized with inverted chords (for better acoustical effect).

Before harmonizing melodies with inverted chords it would be helpful to practice this chord progression (L.H. alone) in the tonic key of each new song:

$(I, IV^6_4, V^6_5, I) - (V^4_2/IV, IV_6, V^4_2/V, V_6, V7, I) - (ii6, I^6_4, V7, I)$

EXAMPLE:

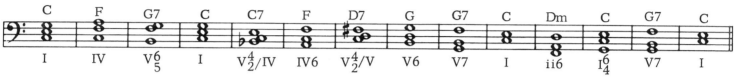

## 22. O CHRISTMAS TREE

German Carol

## 23. FOLK SONG

## 24. FOLK SONG

## 25. FOLK SONG

American

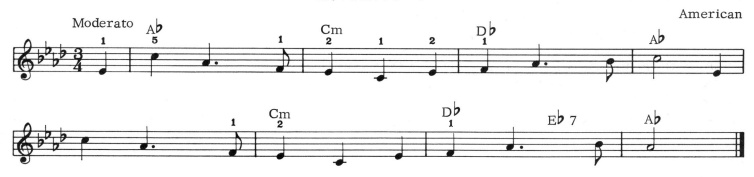

## 26. FOLK SONG

American

## 27. THE ASH GROVE

Welsh

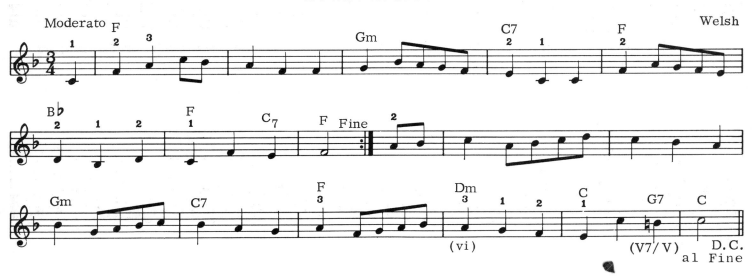

## 28. FOLK SONG (BLUE BELLS OF SCOTLAND)

Scottish

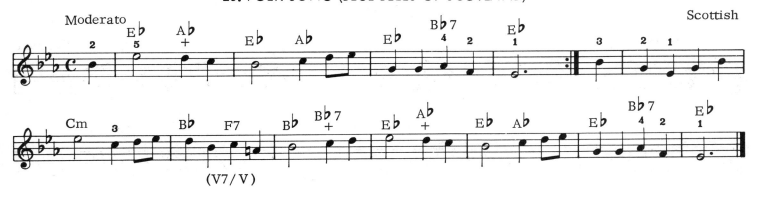

# Unit 15

## 29. BRING BACK MY BONNIE TO ME

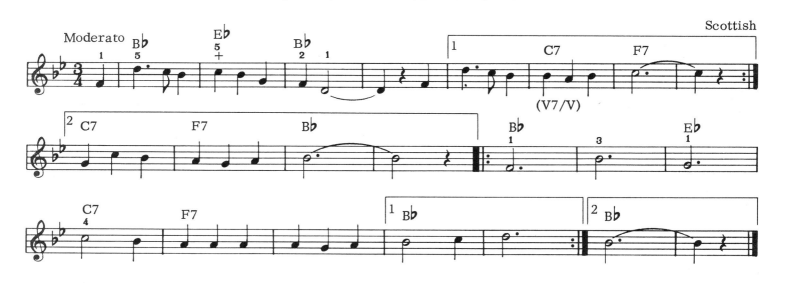

## 30. HOME ON THE RANGE

## 31. FOLK SONG

## 32. JINGLE BELLS

## 33. IT CAME UPON THE MIDNIGHT CLEAR

# Unit 15

### 34. SYMPHONY NO. 8 "UNFINISHED"
(first movement, second theme)

### 35. MAZURKA (Op. 68, No. 3)
(Polish folk dance)

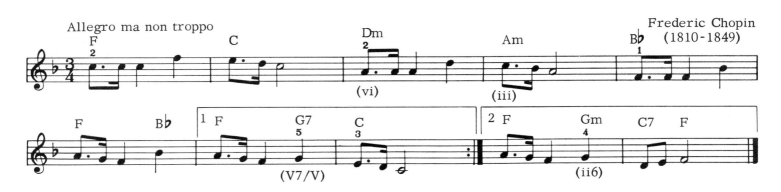

### 36. FÜR ELISE

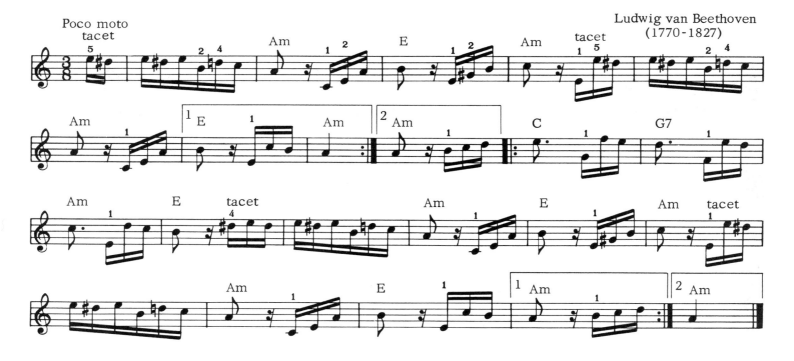

## 37. DIXIE

Dan D. Emmett

(V7/V)

## 38. ALL THROUGH THE NIGHT

Welsh

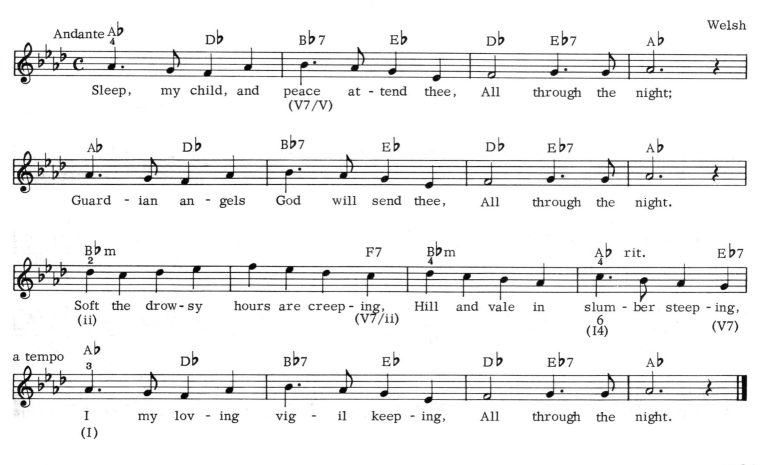

Sleep, my child, and peace at - tend thee, All through the night;
(V7/V)

Guard - ian an - gels God will send thee, All through the night.

Soft the drow - sy hours are creep - ing, Hill and vale in slum - ber steep - ing,
(ii) (V7/ii) (I4) (V7)

a tempo

I my lov - ing vig - il keep - ing, All through the night.
(I)

# Unit 15
## REVIEW QUIZ No. 9

I. Write the correct harmony to the following melody. Use the
ii chord (ii6). Play the melody and harmony together.

German

EXAMPLE: Eb ___ Fm ___ ___ ___ ___ ___ ___ ___ ___

II. Write the correct harmony to the following melody. Use V7/IV
(brief modulation). Play the melody and harmony together.

German

III. Write the correct harmony to the following melody. Use
V7/V. Play the melody and harmony together.

Mexican

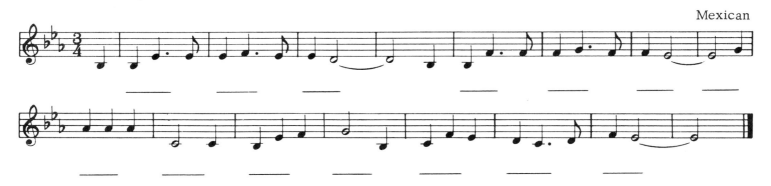

IV. Write the inversions for the following Major chords.

EXAMPLE:

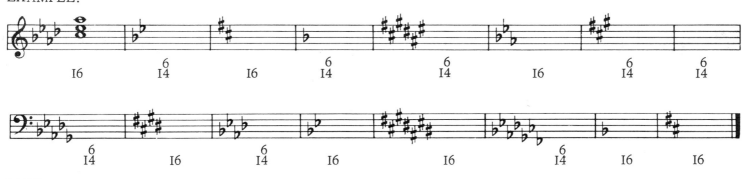

# SECTION FOUR

## PIANO LITERATURE, TECHNIQUE and STYLE

PIANO (19th Century)
Photo courtesy of the Metropolitan Museum of Art, Gift of
George Lowther, 1906. This instrument was built in the United
States by Nunns and Clark during the 19th century.

PIANO (20th Century)
A modern Bosendorfer Concert Grand (Austrian manufacture)
awaiting a 1968 audience in the Royal Festival Hall, London.

TENUTO ( ten.) means to hold the note for its full value.  It
also means to give stress to the note or give a slight accent:

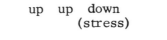 — (tenuto mark)

up   up   down
(stress)

## 1. FOLK DANCE

Béla Bartók
(1881-1945)

## 2. MARCH

Daniel Gottlieb Türk
(1756-1813)

## 3. FIRST DANCE

Allegro

Dmitri Kabalevsky
(1904-1987)

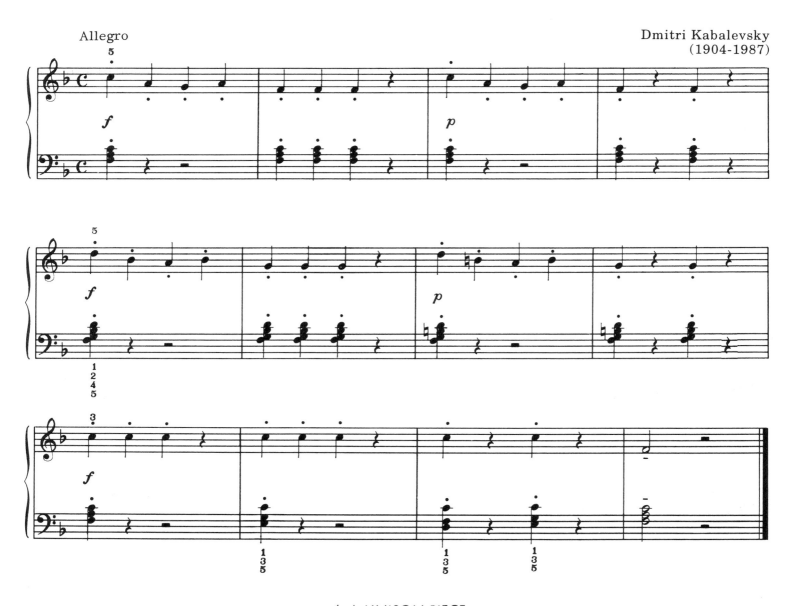

## 4. A UNISON PIECE

Moderato
(D minor)

Dmitri Kabalevsky

Dmitri Kabalevsky

# 6. A BLEAK DAY

Dmitri Kabalevsky

Andante
(B minor)

cantando

mf

Most of the keyboard music written during the Baroque period (1600-1750) was intended to be performed on the HARPSICHORD (the French *clavecin*, the Italian *cembalo*, or *clavicembalo*). The harpsichord was the main forerunner of the modern piano. (The piano was invented in 1709 by the Florentine instrument maker, Bartolomeo Cristofori, and he called it *gravicembalo col piano e forte*, meaning, *harpsichord with soft and loud*.) The main difference in the mechanism between the harpsichord and the piano is that the string of the harpsichord is plucked with a quill, whereas the piano string is hit by a hammer thrown up by the depressed key (as is the CLAVICHORD, another forerunner of the piano).

Much of the keyboard music during this early period was written in collections called dance suites. The DANCE SUITE is an extended instrumental composition consisting of a series of short dances intended to be performed as a whole. The standard dances (or movements) of these seventeenth century keyboard suites consisted of the Allemande, Courante, Sarabande and Gigue. Often a prelude preceded the Allemande, and frequently other movements (such as Gavottes, Bourrées, Minuets, etc.) were interpolated between the Sarabande and Gigue. Most dance movements were written in binary form.

BINARY FORM (or bipartite form) is a musical structure in which balance is obtained by a second section answering the first. This double period form: ‖: A :‖: B :‖ was standard compositional practice for composers of suites (or separate dance movements) during the sixteenth and seventeenth centuries and continued well into the eighteenth century. Notice the use of binary form in some of the following Baroque compositions.

COUNTERPOINT is a term derived from the Latin *punctum contra punctum* (note against note), which originally referred to the setting of voice against voice. It is the art of combining musical voices (or parts) in such a way that they are independent and yet related melodically, harmonically and rhythmically. Notice the effective use of counterpoint in the following Baroque compositions.

## 7. ALLEMANDE

The ALLEMANDE was an old dance form generally assumed to be a German dance, because the name Allemande in French means "German." The Allemande is frequently the first movement in a dance suite and is in 4/4 meter.

## 8. MARCH

Tempo di marcia

Michael Praetorius
(1571 - 1621)

## 9. MINUET

Moderato

Johann Christoph Friedrich Bach
(1732 - 1795)

A SEQUENCE is a repetition of a melodic phrase either higher or lower. Notice the continued use of sequential patterns (symmetrical groupings) throughout the composition. Stress the sequence in measures 7 and 8 (repetition of measures 5 and 6 a tone lower) by the indicated dynamics (*f*-*p* effect).

Release each phrase-ending with a smooth, graceful, up-wrist motion ( ↑ ) for the desired classical (eighteenth century) effect.

## 10. MINUET IN CLASSIC STYLE

J.W.B.

The GAVOTTE was a dance form that became very popular in Europe during the eighteenth century. It is in alla breve ( ¢ ) meter and characteristically begins phrases in mid-measure:

Count    3    4      1  (2)    3    4      1  (2)

## 11. GAVOTTE

Georg Philipp Telemann
(1681 - 1767)

A TRIPLET is a three note figure played in the place of two.

EXAMPLE:

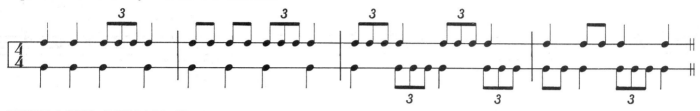

Count:    Quarter    trip - o - let  trip - o - let    two  8ths  half note

Count:       1          2        3         1    2   (3)

Clap the rhythm pattern below, one person clap the rhythm on top, another the rhythm on the bottom.

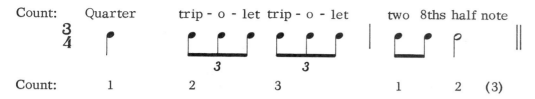

TERRACED DYNAMICS is a term connected with old music and means the direct juxtaposition of loud and soft (forte, piano) without intermediary crescendos or decrescendos.

An early example of this antiphonal effect is Giovanni Gabrieli's (1557-1612) Sonata *pian e forte* which opposes different instrumental choirs.

Use the *una corda* pedal (left pedal) for the sudden *(subito)* piano effect, in measures 6 (repeat of 5), 11-12 (repeat of 9-10), 14 (repeat of 13).

## 12. MINUET

Georg Philipp Telemann
(1681 - 1767)

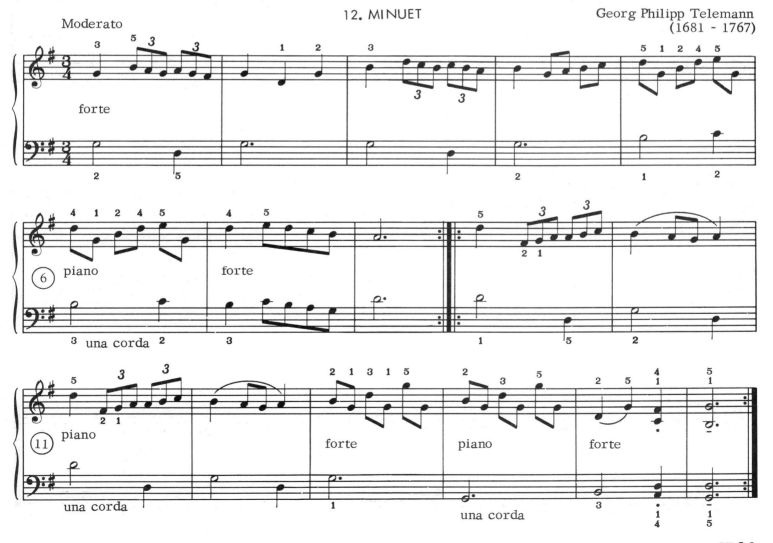

Dmitri Shostakovich
(1906-1975)

Allegro

A SILENT FINGER CHANGE (or finger substitution) is often needed (as in measure 10) to connect legato notes that cannot be reached. Hold the key down and change fingers while holding.

EXAMPLE:

## 14. WALTZ

Dmitri Shostakovich

GP23

TWO CANONS

CANON is a Latin word meaning law or rule. The musical implication is a composition in which strict imitation between two or more voices is the predominant feature.

Two famous examples of compositions employing canons are: Bach's *Goldberg Variations* and Franck's *Sonata in A Major for Violin and Piano* (last movement).

CANON I

(Second time through, use the una corda pedal.)

CANON II

Practice the two studies below first HANDS SEPARATELY, then together. Lift each hand at the end of the slur, but *do not* lift the other hand at the same time. Coordination between hands is a problem, but facility will be acquired with thorough drill.

Play through first using a legato touch, then play a second time using a staccato touch. Transpose chromatically upward to all other keys.

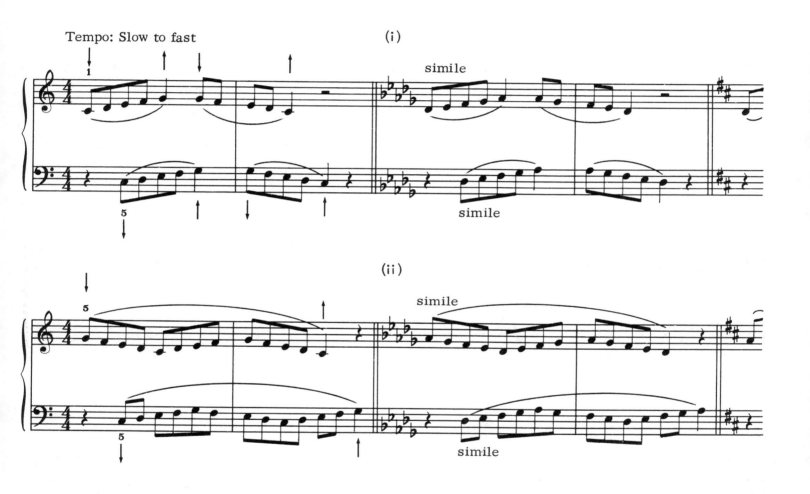

## EXERCISE: LEGATO DOUBLE THIRDS

Keep a good hand position with curved fingers. Change smoothly (legato) from one third to another. Transpose to all other keys.

148

8va means to play an octave higher (above staff) or lower (below staff) than written. It is meant for one staff only. In the composition below only the Right Hand is to be played an octave higher for the third and fourth lines.

## 15. THE FIFERS

Jean François Dandrieu
(1682–1738)

GP23

Practice the two preparatory exercises below. The first is for
facility with repeated notes; the second uses the grace note
(acciacatura: played quickly; literally "crushed" into the main
note) in a five note figure.

PREPARATORY EXERCISES

16. MINUET

Johann Christian Bach
(1735 - 1782)

Allegretto

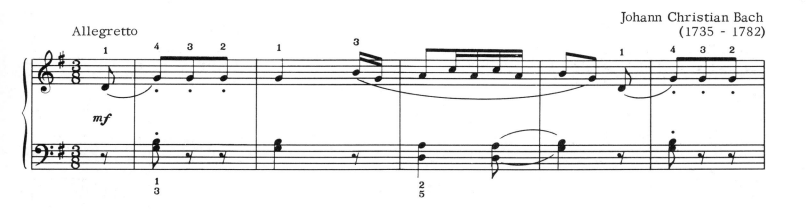

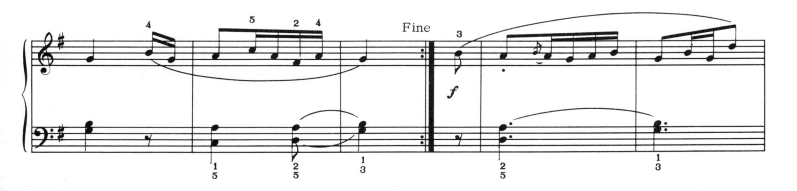

Practice the exercises below for continued facility in changing to new chord positions. Play all exercises *both* up and down as indicated on the first line. Also practice with minor triads in the same fashion. Transpose chromatically upward to all other keys.

(i) BLOCK CHORDS

simile

(ii) BROKEN CHORDS

(iii) STACCATO CHORDS (two's)

(iv) STACCATO CHORDS (three's)

(v) BROKEN CHORDS

R.H.

L.H.

(vi) BROKEN CHORDS

R.H.

L.H.

The composition below is a theme Beethoven used for a set of
variations. The theme is taken from an Arietta (little aria) from
the opera *La Molinara* by Giovanni Paisiello (1740-1816), and is
titled: *Nel cor piu non mi sento* (Why feels my heart so dormant).

Practice the L.H. first with block chords. Play the R.H. alone.
Play the R.H. with the L.H. using block chords. Finally play as
written.

Notice the sequence in measures 11 and 12 (repeat of 9 and 10).
Play measures 11 and 12 at a lower dynamic level because the
sequence is stated a whole tone lower.

18. THEME

Ludwig van Beethoven
(1770–1827)

152

BAGATELLE (from the French) literally means a trifle, and is the name frequently given to short musical compositions.

The correct *balance* is important in this piece; the chords in the L.H. should not over-power the melody in the R.H.

## 19. BAGATELLE

Moderato

Antonio Diabelli
(1781 - 1858)

# MINOR SCALES

A minor scale is derived from its RELATIVE Major scale. It is termed relative because both scales share the same key signature. The minor scale is built on the sixth step of the Major scale, and this form of minor is called *natural* or *pure* minor mode.

## I. NATURAL MINOR SCALE

EXAMPLE: F Major Scale

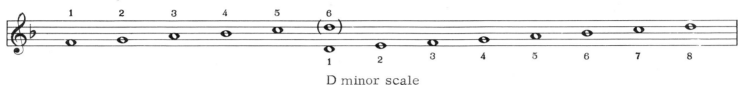

D minor scale

The HARMONIC MINOR SCALE is the most frequently used of the three forms of minor. This scale uses the same notes as the natural minor scale with the exception of the seventh degree of the scale. This change of one note cannot be written into the key signature, but will always appear in the scale as an accidental. To construct the harmonic minor scale RAISE THE SEVENTH DEGREE OF THE SCALE ONE HALF STEP.

## II. HARMONIC MINOR SCALE

EXAMPLE: G minor scale                     Raised 7th

The MELODIC MINOR SCALE is the next most frequently used of the minor scales. This scale consists of two parts: one form of the scale is used ascending and another is used descending. To construct the melodic minor scale RAISE THE SIXTH AND SEVENTH DEGREES OF THE SCALE ONE HALF STEP ASCENDING, AND LOWER THE SIXTH AND SEVENTH DEGREES, DESCENDING.

## III. MELODIC MINOR SCALE

ASCENDING                                  DESCENDING

Raised 6th & 7th        Lowered 7th & 6th

EXAMPLE: G minor scale

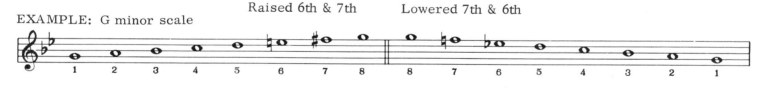

## IDENTIFYING MINOR KEY SIGNATURES

Both the Major scale and its relative minor scale use the same key signature. Therefore the key signature alone does not determine whether the piece is in Major or minor. Always look at the first and last notes (or chords) of a composition for Major or minor scale notes. If the composition has a minor sound, determine its minor key name with this rule: count up a major sixth from the Major key note, or (easier) COUNT DOWN 3 HALF STEPS FROM THE MAJOR KEY. Always end TWO ALPHABET LETTERS LOWER THAN THE MAJOR KEY. This will be the name of the relative minor key.

EXAMPLE:                                    EXAMPLE:

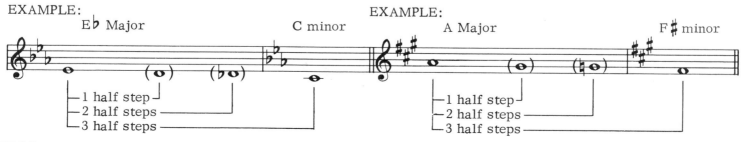

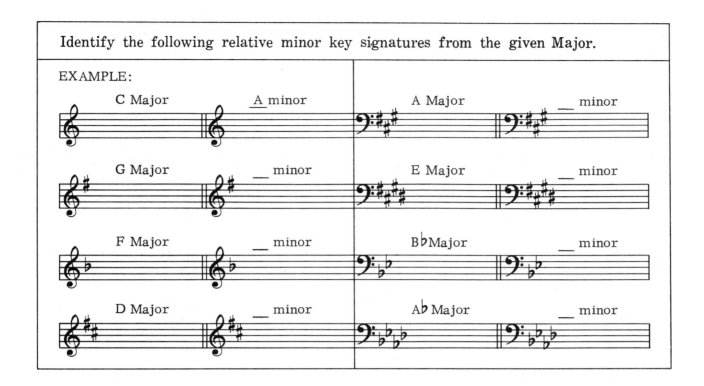

## THE FINGERING FOR MINOR SCALES BEGINNING ON WHITE KEYS
### (Harmonic form)

The fingering is the SAME for both the Major and minor scales beginning on white keys. Major and minor scales beginning on the same note are termed PARALLEL Major and minor.

Play the C minor scale, as given in the example below, both ascending and descending (read the finger numbers backwards for descending) first with the Right Hand and then with the Left Hand. MEMORIZE THIS FINGERING PATTERN.

Write the notes and fingerings for the scales of G, D, A and E minor in the space provided. Then play these in order. Notice the CHANGE OF FINGERING in the Left Hand for the B minor scale, and in the Right Hand for the F minor scale.

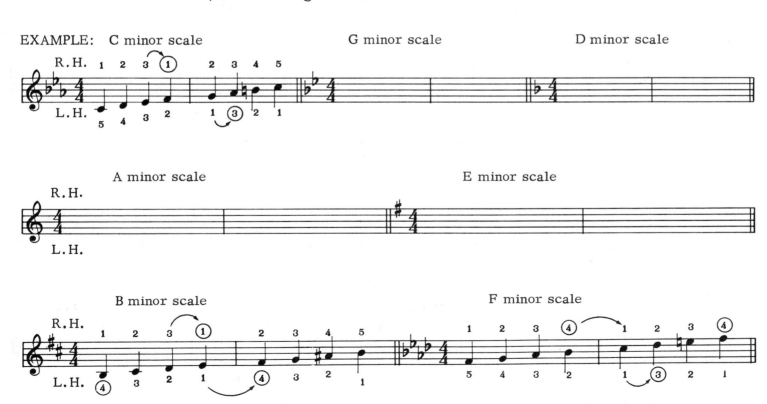

PORTAMENTO (or PORTATO) means slightly disconnected tones in piano music (neither staccato nor legato) and is written:

The first phrase would look this way if the portato were written out:

Practice the phrasing in Bach's compositions in a similar manner and use portamento touch rather than staccato for note separation.

### 21. MINUET IN G MINOR

Johann Sebastian Bach
(1685-1750)

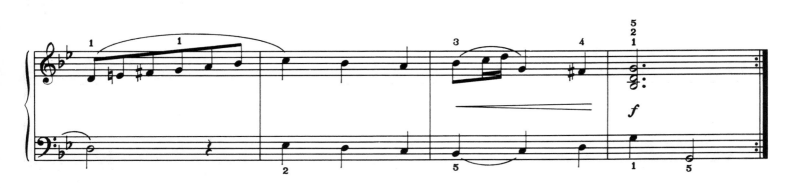

# 22. MINUET IN G MAJOR

Johann Sebastian Bach

Johann Sebastian Bach

Allegro maestoso

A SONATINA (little sonata) is an instrumental composition of abbreviated length, and is a modified replica of a sonata. Sonatina form is distinguished from sonata-allegro form chiefly by the abbreviation or the absence of a development section.

SONATA means "sound piece" and is one of the highest developments of musical form. The typical sonata form (really sonata-allegro form) is an instrumental composition with a ternary formation. Its three parts are known as the *exposition* (A), *development* (B), and *recapitulation* (A2).

## 24. SONATINA
### Op. 157, No. 1

Fritz Spindler
(1817-1905)

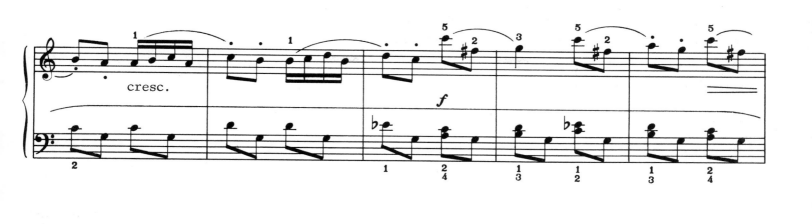

# TWO VELOCITY STUDIES

## FOR THE RIGHT HAND

Carl Czerny
(1791-1857)

## FOR THE LEFT HAND

Allegro

Robert Schumann
(1810-1856)

# 26. LITTLE SONG
## Op. 98

Alexander Gretchaninoff
(1864-1956)

Moderato

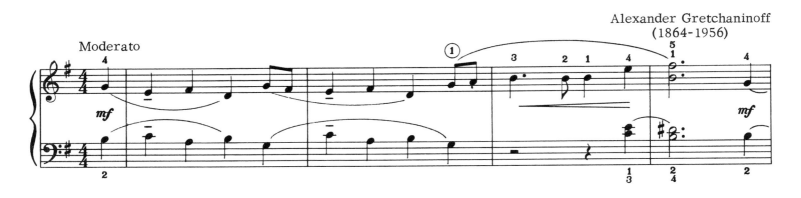

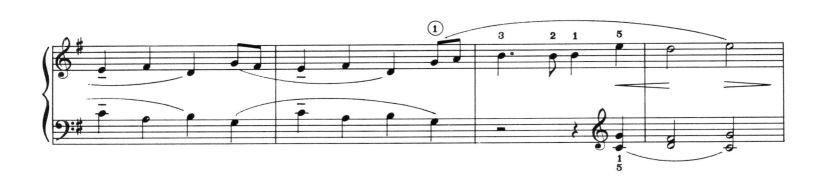

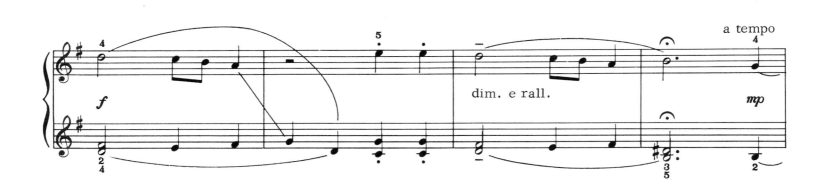

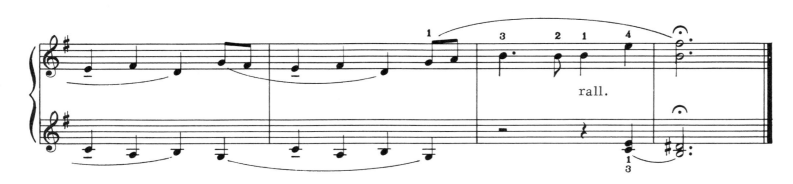

## 27. WALTZ

Dmitri Kabalevsky
(1904-1987)

## 28. FIRST IMMORTELLE

Duet
Secondo

Fritz Spindler
(1817-1905)

## 28. FIRST IMMORTELLE

Duet
Primo

Fritz Spindler
(1817-1905)

A DIMINISHED triad is comprised of tones in a succession of
minor thirds (minor third: three half steps). A diminished triad
has a minor third, and a diminished fifth (lowered one half step).

Notice the diminished triad in the *Etude* below (in measure 11-12).

### 29. ETUDE

Louis Köhler
(1820-1836)
Arr. by J.W.B.

An AUGMENTED triad is comprised of a major third and an augmented fifth (raised one half step).

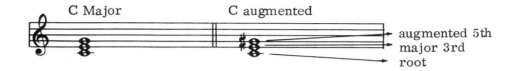

Locate all of the augmented triads in the composition below.

### 30. SONATINA

Jacob Schmitt
(1803-1853)

# FOUR CHORD STUDY

Learn this chord progression for all keys:
Major — Augmented (Augmented) — Major — Minor — Diminished

# THE CADENCE

A CADENCE is the close of a musical phrase. The most common type of cadence is from dominant (which is an active chord) to tonic (which is a passive chord). This is called an *authentic cadence.*

Learn the three possible positions for the authentic cadence notated in the exercise below. Practice this pattern in all keys and be able to play it by memory.

## EXERCISE: AUTHENTIC CADENCE

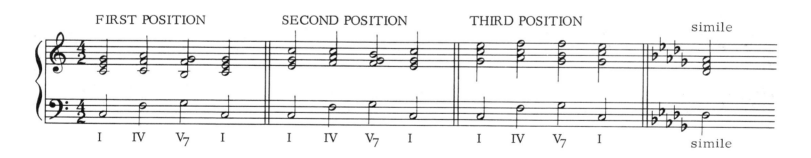

# CHORD RECOGNITION

Name the following chords.

EXAMPLE:

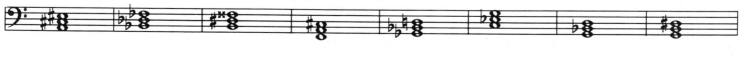

# PREPARATORY EXERCISES

In the exercise below create the effect of a smooth legato by connecting the top notes of the sixths (5-4 or 4-5) and slide the thumb as smoothly as possible.

Practice this exercise for legato pairs of fingers (thirds).

## 31. MINUET

Ignaz Joseph Pleyel
(1757-1831)

# THE FINGERING FOR FOUR-NOTE CHORDS

A FOUR-NOTE CHORD has almost the same sound as a triad, the only difference being an additional root tone added on top of a triad:

The general rule for the fingering is:

### RIGHT HAND
When there is an interval of a *fourth* between the top two notes, use the *third* finger for the third note of the chord:

When there is an interval of a *third* between the top two notes, use the *fourth* finger for the third tone of the chord:

### LEFT HAND
When there is an interval of a *fourth* between the bottom two notes, use the *third* finger for the second tone of the chord:

When there is an interval of a *third* between the bottom two notes, use the *fourth* finger for the second tone of the chord:

Practice the following four-note chords for the correct fingerings.

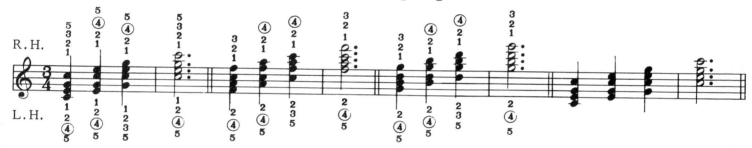

## PRACTICE SUGGESTIONS FOR PASTORAL (No. 32)

Notice the recurring patterns in this composition: The first four measures are repeated once (measures 5-8), then repeated again (measures 15-18).

A sequence occurs in measures 11 and 12 which is a repetition of measures 9 and 10 a whole tone lower.

Practice the following Right Hand preparatory exercises for quick comprehension of the melodic outline.

Practice the following Left Hand preparatory exercise for the pattern that occurs in measure 14. This figure is perhaps the most difficult for the Left Hand and will require extra drill.

### PREPARATORY EXERCISES

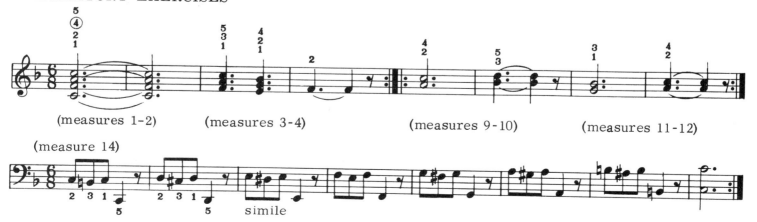

## 32. PASTORAL

Johann Philipp Kirnberger
(1721-1783)

## 33. MINUET IN RONDO FORM

Jean Philippe Rameau
(1683-1764)

OSTINATO is an Italian word meaning obstinate, continual, or unceasing, and is a name given to a frequently recurring pattern, usually in the bass *(basso ostinato)*.

In the composition below the steadily repeated bass tone ("g") produces the effect of a "drone" (the pipe that sounds one note continuously in the bagpipe), and is referred to as *drone bass*. These two terms, basso ostinato and drone bass, have similar meanings.

## 34. MUSETTE

Louis Claude Daquin
(1694-1772)

The ALBERTI BASS is a bass figure of broken chords, and is named after an early eighteenth century composer, Domenico Alberti (born 1710), who used figures of this kind in his sonatas:

Practice the three studies below for facility using this type of broken-chord figure. Note the change in the V7 chord in the first and second endings.

Transpose to all other keys.

(i)

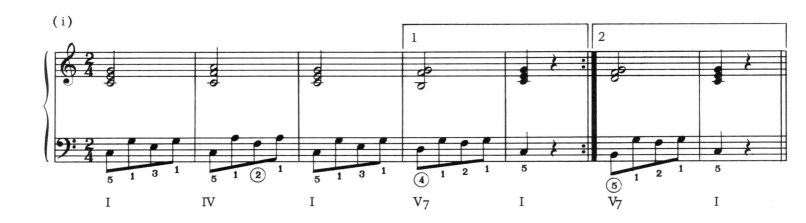

(ii)

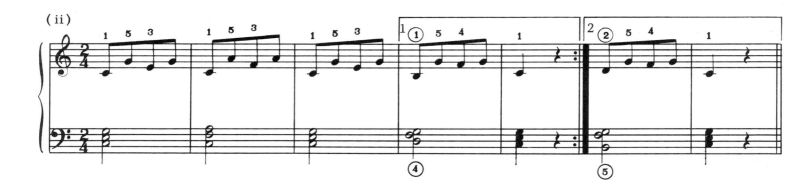

(iii)

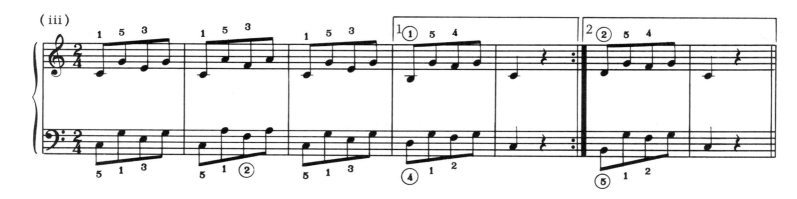

Note: All three studies may be played at the same time for class use as ensemble practice.

D. S. (DAL SEGNO) means to repeat from the sign (%) and stop at Fine.

## 35. ETUDE

J. W. B.

## THE CHROMATIC SCALE: CONTRARY MOTION

178

## PRACTICE PROCEDURE

First play the L.H. alone with block chords in place of the broken chord figure. Then play the R.H. alone (notice the change of fingers for the repeated notes). Then play the R.H. and L.H. together using block chords in the L.H. Finally play as written.

**36.** Theme from SYMPHONY IN G MINOR (K. 550)

(first movement)

Wolfgang Amadeus Mozart
(1756–1791)
Arr. by J.W.B.

Identify the following minor key signatures.

EXAMPLE:

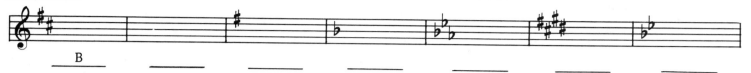

B

## THE FINGERING FOR MINOR SCALES BEGINNING ON BLACK KEYS
### (Harmonic form)

Compare the fingerings for the parallel Major and minor scales beginning on black keys. The fingering is the same except for these four changes:

- B♭ Major, L.H. 3 2 1 4 3 2 1 3
- B♭ minor, L.H. 2 1 3 2 1 4 3 2

- D♭ Major, R.H. 2 3 1 2 3 4 1 2
- C♯ minor, R.H. 3 4 1 2 3 1 2 3

- E♭ Major, L.H. 3 2 1 4 3 2 1 3
- E♭ minor, L.H. 2 1 4 3 2 1 3 2

- G♭ Major, R.H. 2 3 4 1 2 3 1 2
- F♯ minor, R.H. 3 4 1 2 3 1 2 3

Practice the five minor scales below both ascending and descending (read the finger numbers backwards for descending) first with the R.H., then the L.H., then both hands together. MEMORIZE THESE FINGERING PATTERNS.

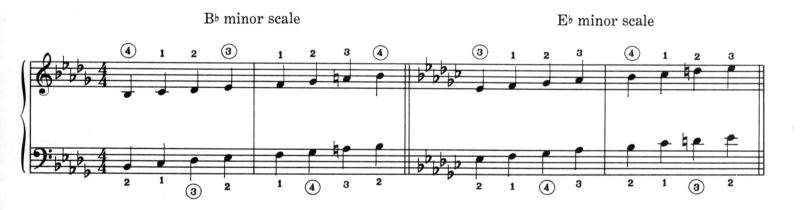

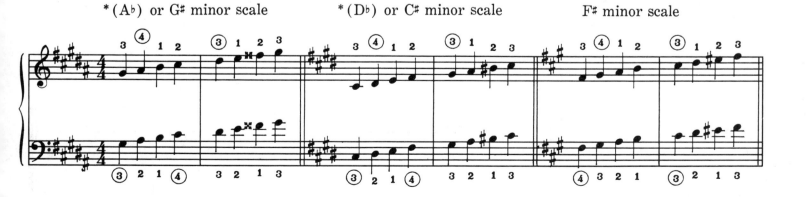

*(Review) The term ENHARMONIC is used to denote two letter names having the same pitch.

## 37. MERRY PEASANT
### (returning from his work)

Robert Schumann
(1810-1856)

## 38. MINUET IN F *(K. 2)

Allegretto

Wolfgang Amadeus Mozart
(1756-1791)

*The K after a Mozart work is an abbreviation for Köchel (sounds like: KUR shell), the man who catalogued Mozart's compositions. Mozart wrote more than 600 works, and when he died his manuscripts were in such a mixed-up state that we are indebted to Köchel for sorting them out. The Minuet, K. 2, is one of Mozart's first works composed when he was only six.

The WHOLE TONE SCALE is a scale composed of only six tones arranged in a series a whole step apart.

## WHOLE TONE SCALE

ASCENDING          DESCENDING

This scale was frequently used by composers in the impressionistic period (early twentieth century) such as Debussy (1862-1918) and Ravel (1875-1937).

Note the use of the whole tone scale in the following composition in measures 14-15.

### 39. WALTZ

J. W. B.

(melody)

# THE SYNCOPATED PEDAL

A smooth legato effect is necessary for playing chorals. This is accomplished at the piano in two ways: first by connecting the fingering by means of finger substitution (changing fingers while holding down a key, or keys), and secondly by using a syncopated pedal to bind together similar harmonies.

The SYNCOPATED PEDAL (or LEGATO PEDAL) is effected by a change of pedal on the beat (or with each new change in harmony) in the following manner: Push the sostenuto pedal (right pedal) down with the first note at the same time. Thereafter, play the key and release the pedal on the beat, then push the pedal down again after the key has been played as shown in the following rhythm.

| Beat: | 1 | 2 | 3 | 4 | 1 | 2 | 3 | 4 |
|-------|----|----|--------|----|------|----|------|---|
| Pedal: | down | up | down up | | down | up | down |

Practice the scale below using the pedal as described. Use the third finger (either hand), then play other scales in the same manner. Say the words "up-down" in a steady, even rhythm on the beat as each note is played.

## 40. CHORAL

J. W. B.

## 42. CHORAL

GP23

# 43. HUNGARIAN FOLK SONG

Béla Bartók
(1881-1945)

*America, America the Beautiful,* and *The Star-Spangled Banner* are sung with such frequency that these three songs should be memorized and ready to play at all times.

When committing a piece "to memory" be aware of a number of things:

1. Look for recurring patterns (ascending or descending figures).
2. Memorize in phrases (first with the R.H., then with the L.H., then both together).
3. Always use the *same* fingering to assure correct kinesthetic response.
4. Be aware of the harmonic progressions.
5. Create a "mental picture" of how it would "feel" to play each phrase.

Memorize the following three songs.

## 44. AMERICA

Samuel F. Smith

Henry Carey

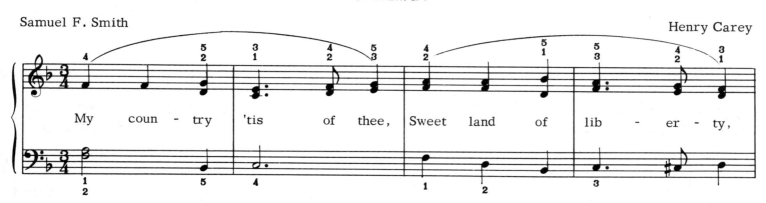

My coun - try 'tis of thee, Sweet land of lib - er - ty,

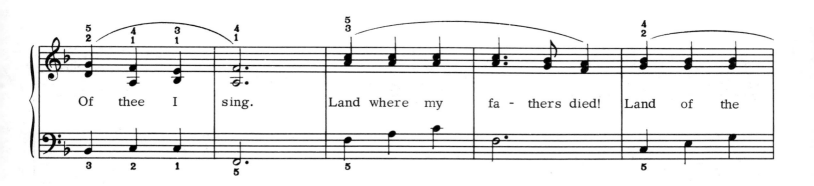

Of thee I sing. Land where my fa - thers died! Land of the

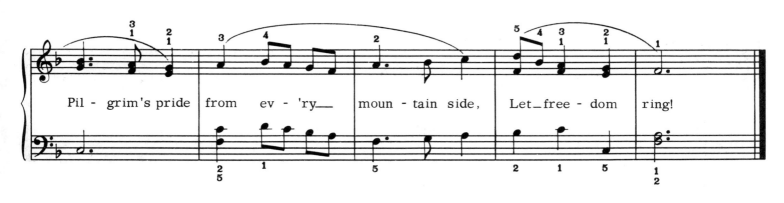

Pil - grim's pride from ev - 'ry___ moun - tain side, Let_free - dom ring!

188

## 45. AMERICA THE BEAUTIFUL

Katherine Lee Bates

Samuel A. Ward

GP23

## 45. THE STAR-SPANGLED BANNER

Francis Scott Key

John Stafford Smith

With spirit

190

This composition is an excellent study for quick changing triads
in all positions. Think ahead for each chord change and anticipate each new hand position.

PEDAL POINT is a term used to designate a note (or notes)
sustained in the bass part, over which harmonies change in the
upper parts.

47. MARCH

Alexander Gretchaninoff
(1864-1956)

Practice the following harmonic progressions using the correct fingering. Connect the top note of the right hand triad (soprano voice), often using finger substitution for the legato effect. Practice first without the pedal, then add a syncopated sostenuto pedal for maximum legato.

Play the progressions in the written keys and then transpose to all other keys. Also play in minor keys.

TONIC — DOMINANT

TONIC — SUBDOMINANT — DOMINANT

TONIC — SUPERTONIC — DOMINANT

TONIC — SUPERTONIC

TONIC — SUBMEDIANT — SUPERTONIC — DOMINANT

Practice the following chord drills first with the R.H., then the L.H., then play both hands together an octave apart. Transpose chromatically upward to all other keys.

### TRIADS OF THE MAJOR SCALES (BLOCK FORM)
(i)

Major minor minor Major Major minor diminished Major

I   ii   iii   IV   V   vi   vii°   I

### BROKEN-CHORD FORM
(ii)

(iii)        (iv)        (v)

### TRIADS AND INVERSIONS OF THE MAJOR SCALES (BLOCK FORM)
(vi)

### BROKEN-CHORD FORM
(vii)        (viii)        (ix)        (x)

### FOUR-NOTE CHORDS (BLOCK FORM)     BROKEN-CHORD FORM
(xi)        (xii)        (xiii)

### SEVENTH CHORDS (BLOCK FORM)     BROKEN-CHORD FORM
(xiv)        (xv)        (xvi)

### DOMINANT SEVENTH CHORDS AND INVERSIONS (BLOCK FORM) BROKEN-CHORD FORM
(xvii)        (xviii)        (xix)

### DIMINISHED SEVENTH CHORDS AND INVERSIONS (BLOCK FORM) BROKEN-CHORD FORM
(xx)        (xxi)        (xxii)

GP23

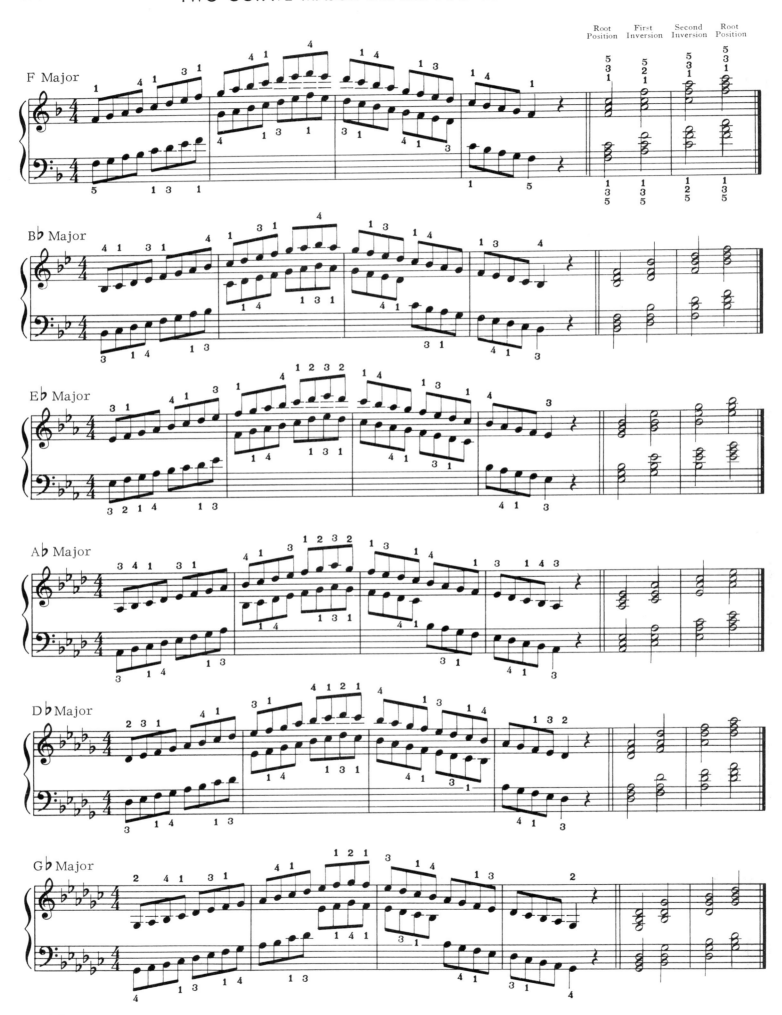

(Harmonic Form)

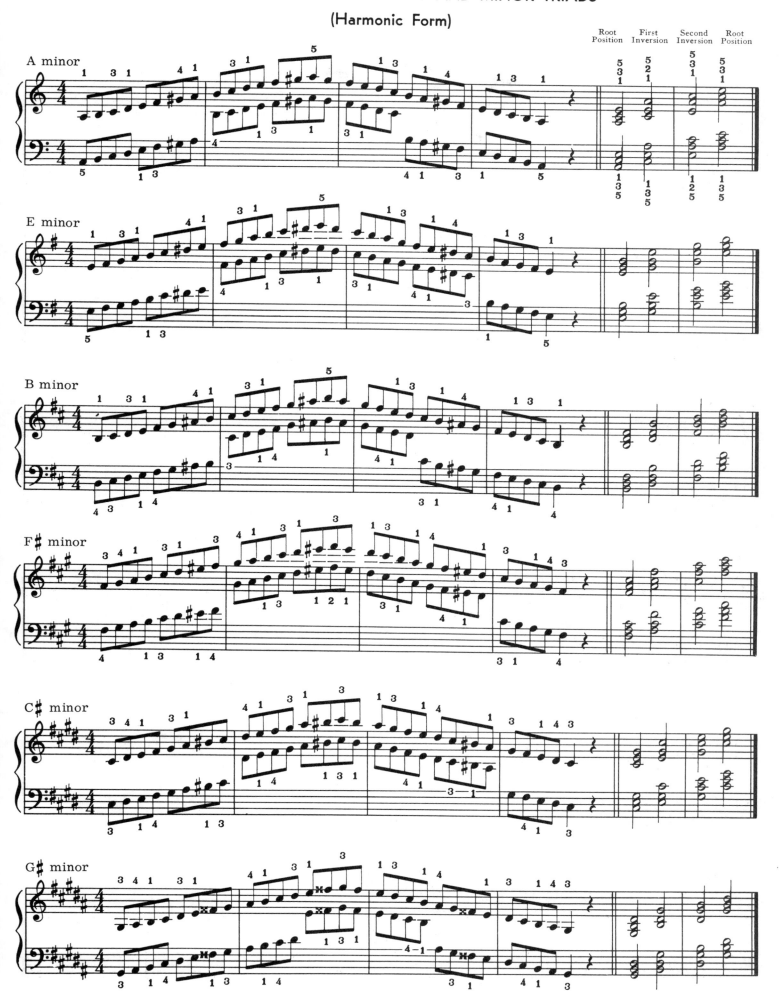

# TWO OCTAVE MINOR SCALES AND MINOR TRIADS
## (Harmonic Form)

# APPENDIXES

PIANO (Electronic)
A modern electronic piano manufactured in Germany by the
firm of Hohner. Electronic keyboard instruments have achieved
an especially wide acceptance in the fields of popular music
and class piano instruction during the mid-20th century.

# APPENDIX A
## A BRIEF THEORY OUTLINE

This outline is offered only as an insight to materials discussed during theoretical studies, and is not designed to supplant a formal course in theory.

## SCALES

A SCALE is an arbitrary arrangement of tones in a series of increasing (ascending) or decreasing (descending) pitches. The various scales may be identified by the number of pitches used and their intervallic relationships. A scale may have the same tones for both ascending and descending or may have one series of tones ascending and another descending. Scales are constructed with half steps (½ step: the smallest interval in Western music), whole steps (two ½ steps), or with larger intervals (1½ steps). In the scales below ⌣ = ½ step, ⌃ = 1½ steps.

## COMMONLY USED SCALES

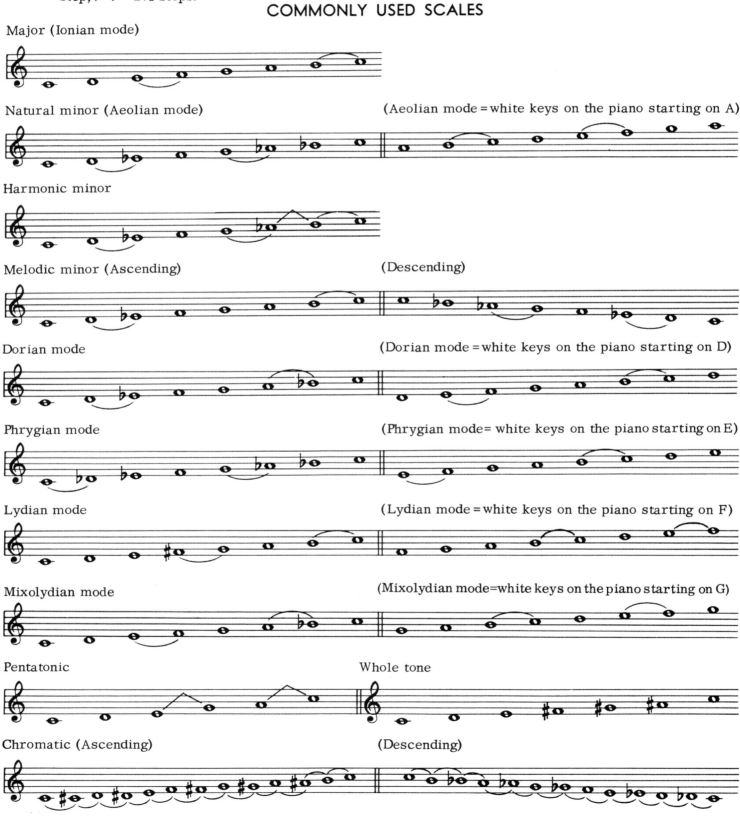

Major (Ionian mode)

Natural minor (Aeolian mode)    (Aeolian mode = white keys on the piano starting on A)

Harmonic minor

Melodic minor (Ascending)    (Descending)

Dorian mode    (Dorian mode = white keys on the piano starting on D)

Phrygian mode    (Phrygian mode= white keys on the piano starting on E)

Lydian mode    (Lydian mode = white keys on the piano starting on F)

Mixolydian mode    (Mixolydian mode=white keys on the piano starting on G)

Pentatonic    Whole tone

Chromatic (Ascending)    (Descending)

It is customary to refer to the scale degrees by Roman numerals:

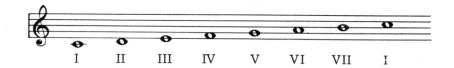

Scale degrees are also referred to by the following names:

I. Tonic (the key-note)
II. Supertonic (one step above the tonic)
III. Mediant (halfway from tonic to dominant)
IV. Subdominant (as far below the tonic as the dominant is above it)
V. Dominant (a major or "dominant" element in the key)
VI. Submediant (halfway down from tonic to subdominant)
VII. Leading tone (has a melodic tendency towards the tonic)

## INTERVALS

An INTERVAL is the pitch relation or distance between two tones. The various types of intervals are: Major, minor, perfect, augmented, diminished.

## MAJOR AND PERFECT INTERVALS

## CHROMATICALLY ALTERED INTERVALS

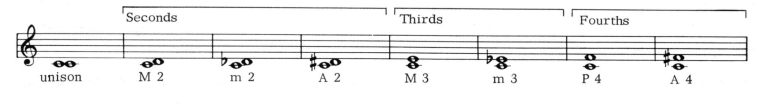

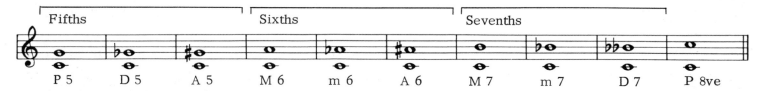

## TYPES OF TRIADS

A TRIAD (three-note chord) is formed by superposition of thirds. There are four kinds of triads, classified according to the nature of the intervals formed between the root and the other two tones.

(a) Major triad (Maj.) composed of a major third and perfect fifth
(b) minor triad (min.) composed of a minor third and perfect fifth
(c) augmented triad (aug.) composed of a major third and augmented fifth
(d) diminished triad (dim.) composed of a minor third and diminished fifth

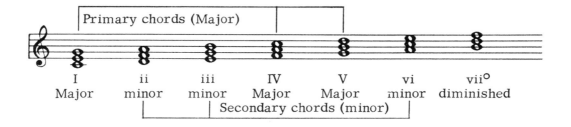

## TYPES OF TRIADS WITHIN THE HARMONIC MINOR SCALE

### FIRST INVERSION TRIADS

An inversion is a rearrangement of the same tones used in the basic chord (root position chord). Triads in first inversion are called chords of the sixth because of the interval of a sixth between the top and bottom notes. The third of the triad is in the bass.

The figured bass (method of musical shorthand) Arabic numerals for first inversion chords are $\frac{6}{3}$ , or simply 6, the third being assumed.

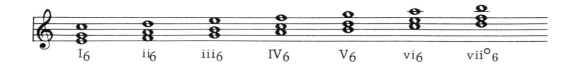

### SECOND INVERSION TRIADS

Triads in second inversion are termed six-four chords because of the interval of a sixth between the top and bottom notes and the fourth between the middle and bottom notes. The fifth of the triad is in the bass.

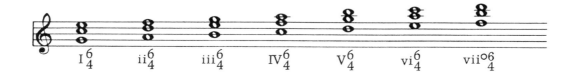

### FOUR-PART HARMONY

Four-part harmony is the basis for most music of the eighteenth and nineteenth centuries. This means a vertical construction of four chord tones (one being doubled in triads), and a horizontal movement of four different melodic voices. Voices refers to the standard vocal quartet: soprano, alto, tenor, bass. However the term 'voices' may also refer to instrumental *parts*. The study of harmony is concerned with the principles that govern the vertical and horizontal movement of these four voices (or parts).

Essentially the spacing of tones within chords is either in *close* or *open* structure. When the three upper voices are as close together as possible (soprano and tenor not exceeding an octave apart), the spacing is called close position. Any spacing that exceeds a distance greater than an octave between soprano and tenor is called open position.

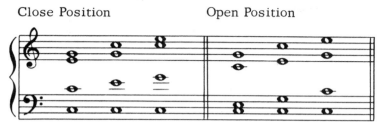

Close Position        Open Position

## DOUBLINGS

It is obvious that one of the three tones in a triad must be doubled to write four-part harmony. The extra tone is usually obtained by doubling the root in root position chords (as in the examples above). Other rules apply for doublings of first and second inversion chords. (Consult a formal theory text.)

## CADENCES

Music is quite analogous to literature because of its essentially linear, horizontal (left to right) motion. The horizontal, melodic movement of music is punctuated by phrases, whereas the vertical (chordal) structure culminates in *cadences* (various points of rest). Below are examples of frequently used cadences.

(a) The *authentic cadence* is comparable to a full stop or a period in punctuation, and consists of a V-I harmonic progression.

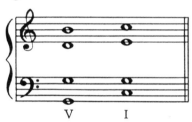

V      I

(b) The *half cadence* acts like a comma, indicating a partial stop in an unfinished statement. It ends on a V chord, however approached.

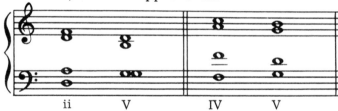

ii    V      IV    V

(c) The *plagal cadence* is the next most frequently used progression for a full stop or final repose after the authentic cadence. It is also the "amen" sound used in hymns and consists of a IV-I progression.

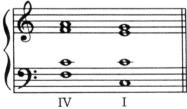

IV    I

(d) The *deceptive cadence* is a frequent substitute for the authentic cadence. As an alternative to V-I, V-vi (deceptive cadence) is often used.

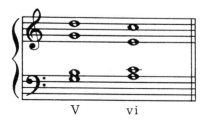

V    vi

# NONHARMONIC TONES (Non-Chord-Tones)

The texture of music is comprised of melodic tones and rhythms which are interwoven. Some of these tones appear as factors of chords and some do not. *Nonharmonic tones* are tones that become foreign to the prevailing harmony during the course of melodic movement. Below are examples of frequently used nonharmonic tones.

(a) A *passing tone* is a dissonant tone (non-chordal tone) interpolated generally between two consonant tones. It usually occurs on a rhythmically weak beat and is approached and left by step without change of direction. The passing tone (or tones) may be either diatonic or chromatic.

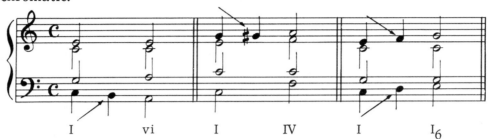

(b) An *auxiliary tone* (also called neighboring tone or embellishment) is a dissonant tone of weak rhythmic value which serves to ornament a stationary tone (either from above or below). It is approached and left by step with change of direction.

(c) An *anticipation*, as its name implies, is an advance sounding of the subsequent tone. It acts as an up-beat to the tone anticipated. It is a dissonant, rhythmically weak tone, usually approached by step, and becomes consonant without moving as the harmony resolves to it.

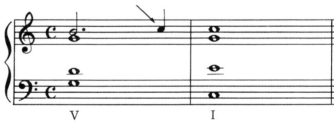

(d) An *escape tone* (or échappée) is a dissonant, rhythmically weak tone, approached by step and left by leap.

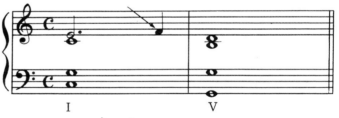

(e) An *appoggiatura* (from the Italian verb *appoggiare*, to lean) is a dissonant tone on a rhythmically strong beat which is usually approached by leap and left by step.

(f) A *suspension* (or retardation) is the prolongation of a chordal tone of which it is a member, into a chord of which it is not a member. The three elements of the suspension are frequently referred to as the *preparation* (consonant tone), *suspension* (dissonant tone on a rhythmically strong beat), and *resolution* (usually by step downward).

A SEVENTH CHORD (four-note chord) is formed by superposing an interval of a third upon a triad. A seventh chord may be constructed on any scale degree, with or without chromatic alterations. The seventh chord built on the fifth of the scale (dominant seventh) is the most frequently used of the seventh chords. All other seventh chords (non-dominant) are termed *secondary sevenths*.

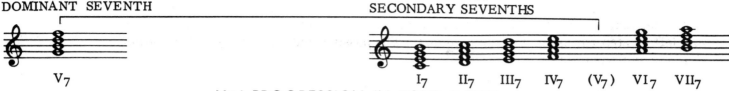

DOMINANT SEVENTH                SECONDARY SEVENTHS

$V_7$           $I_7$   $II_7$   $III_7$   $IV_7$   $(V_7)$   $VI_7$   $VII_7$

## V7-I PROGRESSION IN FOUR PARTS

The natural (or regular) resolution of V7 to I is one of the most fundamental harmonic progressions in music. The tones of the dominant seventh chord have a natural tendency to resolve to the tonic. The root of the chord resolves up a fourth (or down a fifth); the third of the chord (leading tone) usually ascends to the tonic; the fifth of the chord (having no tendency) descends to the tonic; the seventh resolves downward one scale degree to the third of the tonic chord. This results in an incomplete tonic chord in resolution (three roots and one third).

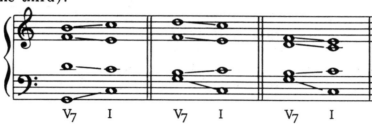

$V_7$   I      $V_7$   I      $V_7$   I

## INVERSIONS OF THE DOMINANT SEVENTH

The *first inversion* of the dominant seventh chord (with the third in the bass) is figured $V_{5 \atop 3}^{6}$; the 3 is often omitted, and the chord is most frequently referred to as $V_{5}^{6}$.

$V_5^6$                 $V_5^6$   I

The *second inversion* of the dominant seventh chord (with the fifth in the bass) is figured $V_{4 \atop 3}^{6}$; the 6 is often omitted, and the chord is most frequently referred to as $V_{3}^{4}$.

$V_3^4$                 $V_3^4$   I

The *third inversion* of the dominant seventh chord (with the seventh in the bass) is figured $V_{4 \atop 2}^{6}$; the 6 is often omitted, and the chord is most frequently referred to as $V_{2}^{4}$, or $V_2$.

$V_2^4$                 $V_2$   $I_6$

## OTHER ASPECTS OF THEORY

Continued theoretical studies would include: irregular resolutions of the V7 chord (and other seventh chords); modulation (discussed briefly on p. 124); diminished seventh chords; ninth, eleventh, thirteenth chords; neapolitan sixth chords; augmented sixth chords; other chromatically altered chords. Consult any of the suggested theory books listed in appendix D for a thorough discussion of all material pertaining to theory.

# APPENDIX B

## A HISTORICAL LISTING OF CONCERT PIANISTS

### THE OLDER GENERATION

Louis Moreau Gottschalk, American (1828-1869)
Anton Rubinstein, Russian (1829-1894)
Amy Fay, American (1844-1928)
Vladimir de Pachmann, Russian (1848-1933)
Ignace Jan Paderewski, Polish (1860-1941)
Moriz Rosenthal, Polish (1862-1946)
Leopold Godowsky, Polish-American (1870-1938)
Sergei Rachmaninoff, Russian (1873-1943)
Josef Lhevinne, Russian-American (1874-1944)
Josef Hofmann, Polish-American (1876-1957)
Alfred Cortot, French (1877-1962)
Ossip Gabrilowitsch, Russian-American (1878-1936)
Wanda Landowska, Polish (1879-1959)
(pianist-harpsichordist)
Edwin Fischer, Swiss (1886-1960)
Myra Hess, English (1890-1966)
Benno Moiseiwitsch, Russian (1890-1963)
Walter Gieseking, German (1895-1956)
Clara Haskil, Rumanian (1895-1960)

### THE MIDDLE GENERATION

Wilhelm Backhaus, German (1884-1969)
Artur Rubinstein, Polish-American (1887-1982)
Jose Iturbi, Spanish-American (1895-1980)
Wilhelm Kempff, German (1895-    )
Alexander Brailowsky, Russian (1896-1976)
Guiomar Novaes, Brazilian (1896-1979)
Robert Casadesus, French (1899-1972)
Cutner Solomon, English (1902-    )
Claudio Arrau, Chilian (1903-    )
Rudoff Serkin, German-American (1903-    )
Vladimir Horowitz, Russian-American (1904-    )
Oscar Levant, American (1906-1972)
Clifford Curzon, English (1907-1982)
Beveridge Webster, American (1908-    )
Alexander Uninsky, Russian-American (1910-1972)
Rudolf Firkusný, Czech (1912-    )
György Sándor, Hungarian-American (1912-    )
Jorge Bolet, Cuban-American (1914-    )
Witold Malcuzynski, Polish (1914-1977)
Sviatoslav Richter, Russian (1915-    )
Rosalyn Tureck, American (1914-    )
Emil Gilels, Russian (1916-    )
Dinu Lipatti, Rumanian (1917-1950)
Arturo Benedetti Michelangeli, Italian (1920-    )
William Kapell, American (1922-1953)

### THE YOUNGER GENERATION

Grant Johannesen, American (1921-    )
Leonard Pennario, American (1924-    )
Eugene Istomin, American (1925-    )
Theodore Lettvin, American (1926-    )
Paul Badura-Skoda, Austrian (1927-    )
Jörg Demus, Austrian (1928-    )
Leon Fleisher, American (1928-    )
Byron Janis, American (1924-    )
Claude Frank, German (1925-    )
David Bar-Illan, Israeli (1930-    )
Friedrich Gulda, Austrian (1930-    )
Ivan Davis, American (1932-    )
Glen Gould, Canadian (1932-    )
John Browning, American (1933-    )
Joseph Banowetz, American (1934-    )
Van Cliburn, American (1934-    )
Philippe Entremont, French (1934-    )
Vladimir Ashkenazy, Russian (1937-    )
James Dick, American (1940-    )
Daniel Barenboim, Argentinian (1942-    )
Lorin Hollander, American (1944-    )
Misha Dichter, American (1945-    )
André Watts, German (1946-    )
Jean-Phillippe Collard, French (1948-    )

# APPENDIX C

## A CHRONOLOGICAL LIST OF KEYBOARD COMPOSERS

**BAROQUE PERIOD (1600-1750)**

Jean Baptiste Lully, French (1632-1687)
Henry Purcell, English (1658-1695)
François Couperin, French (1688-1733)
Georg Philipp Telemann, German (1681-1767)
Jean-Philippe Rameau, French (1683-1764)
Johann Sebastian Bach, German (1685-1750)
Domenico Scarlatti, Italian (1685-1757)
George Frederic Handel, German (1685-1759)

**CLASSICAL PERIOD (1775-1825)**

PRE-CLASSIC KEYBOARD COMPOSERS

Wilhelm Friedemann Bach, German (1710-1784)
Carl Philipp Emanuel Bach, German (1714-1788)
Johann Christian Bach, German (1735-1782)
Johann Philipp Kirnberger, German (1721-1783)

CLASSICAL KEYBOARD COMPOSERS

Franz Joseph Haydn, Austrian (1732-1809)
Muzio Clementi, Italian (1752-1832)
Wolfgang Amadeus Mozart, German (1756-1791)
Daniel Gottlieb Türk, German (1756-1813)
Ludwig van Beethoven, German (1770-1827)
Antonio Diabelli, Italian (1781-1858)
Friedrich Kuhlau, German (1786-1832)

**ROMANTIC PERIOD (1800-1900)**

Franz Schubert, German (1797-1828)
Felix Mendelssohn, German (1809-1847)
Friedrich Burgmüller, German (1806-1874)
Frédéric Chopin, Polish (1810-1849)
Robert Schumann, German (1810-1856)
Franz Liszt, Hungarian (1811-1886)
Stephen Heller, German (1813-1888)
Fritz Spindler, German (1817-1905)
Theodor Kullak, German (1818-1882)
Louis Köhler, German (1820-1886)
Cornelius Gurlitt, German (1820-1901)
Cesar Auguste Franck, French (1822-1890)
Johannes Brahms, German (1833-1897)
Camille Saint-Saens, French (1835-1921)
Modest Mussorgsky, Russian (1839-1881)
Peter Ilyich Tchaikovsky, Russian (1840-1893)
Edvard Grieg, Norwegian (1844-1908)
Vladimir Rebikoff, Russian (1866-1920)

**CONTEMPORARY PERIOD (1900-    )**

Edward MacDowell, American (1861-1908)
Claude Debussy, French (1862-1918)
Alexander Gretchaninoff, Russian (1864-1956)
Alexander Scriabin, Russian (1872-1915)
Max Reger, German (1873-1916)
Sergei Rachmaninoff, Russian (1873-1943)
Arnold Schoenberg, German (1874-1950)
Maurice Ravel, French (1875-1937)
Manuel de Falla, Spanish (1876-1946)
Ernst von Dohnanyi, Hungarian (1877-1960)
Ernest Bloch, Swiss (1880-1959)
Béla Bartók, Hungarian (1881-1945)
Heitor Villa-Lobos, Brazilian (1881-1959)
Joaquin Turina, Spanish (1882-1949)
Igor Stravinsky, Russian (1882-1971)
Sergei Prokofiev, Russian (1891-1952)
Darius Milhaud, French (1892-1974)
Paul Hindemith, German (1895-1963)
George Gershwin, American (1898-1937)
Francis Poulenc, French (1899-1963)
Alexander Tcherepnin, Russian (1899-1977)
Aaron Copland, American (1900-1990)
Aram Khachaturian, Russian (1903-1978)
Dmitri Kabalevsky, Russian (1904-1987)
Dmitri Shostakovich, Russian (1906-1975)
Jean Berger, American (1909-    )
Samuel Barber, American (1901-1981)
Norman Dello Joio, American (1913-    )
Vincent Persichetti, American (1915-1987)

# APPENDIX D

## GENERAL REFERENCE BOOKS ON MUSIC

### PIANO

Oscar Bie, *Pianoforte and Pianoforte Players.* New York: Da Capo Press, 1966.
Abram Chasins, *Speaking of Pianists.* New York: Alfred Knopf, 1961.
James Friskin and Irwin Freundlich, *Music for Piano.* New York: Rinehart, 1954.
Jozsef Gat, *The Technique of the Piano.* Translated by Istvan Kleszky. London: Collet's Holdings Limited, 1965.
John Gillespie, *Five Centuries of Keyboard Music.* Belmont, Calif.: Wadsworth, 1965.
Alice Kern and Helen Titus, *The Teacher's Guidebook to Piano Literature.* Ann Arbor, Mich.: Edwards, 1964.
F. E. Kirby, *A Short History of Keyboard Music.* New York: The Free Press, 1966.
Arthur Loesser, *Men, Women and Pianos.* New York: Simon and Schuster, 1954.
Judith Oringer, *Passion for the Piano.* Los Angeles: Tarcher, Inc., 1983
Harold C. Schoenberg, *The Great Pianists from Mozart to the Present.* New York: Simon and Schuster, 1963.

### INTRODUCTORY BOOKS ON MUSIC

Leonard Bernstein, *The Joy of Music.* New York: Simon and Schuster, 1959.
Guy Bockmon and William Starr, *Scored for Listening.* Alternate ed. New York: Harcourt, Brace and World, Inc., 1964.
Aaron Copland, *What to Listen for in Music.* Rev. ed. New York: McGraw-Hill, 1957.
Joseph Machlis, *The Enjoyment of Music.* Rev. ed. New York: Norton, 1963.
Douglas Moore, A *Guide to Musical Styles.* New York: Norton.
William Newman, *Understanding Music.* 2nd ed., rev. and enl. New York: Harper, 1961.
Edwin Stringham, *Listening to Music Creatively.* 2nd ed. Englewood Cliffs, N.J.: Prentice-Hall, 1959.

### DICTIONARIES AND ENCYCLOPEDIAS

Harold Barlow and Sam Morgenstern, *A Dictionary of Musical Themes.* New York: Crown Publisher, 1948.
Sir George Grove, ed., *The New Grove Dictionary of Music and Musicians.* Edited by Stanley Sadie. 20 vols.
    New York: St. Martin's Press, 1954.
Don Michael Randel, *The New Harvard Dictionary of Music.* Cambridge, Mass.: Harvard University Press, 1986.
Jack Sacher, *Music A to Z.* New York: Grosset and Dunlap, 1963.
Nicolas Slonimsky, *Baker's Biographical Dictionary of Musicians.* 8th ed. New York: Schirmer Books, 1994.
Oscar Thompson, ed., *The International Cyclopedia of Music and Musicians.* 9th ed., edited by Robert Sabin.
    New York: Dodd, Mead, 1964.
J. A. Westrup and F. L. Harrison, *The New College Encyclopedia of Music.* New York: Norton, 1960.

### HISTORIES

William W. Austin, *Music in the 20th Century.* New York: Norton, 1966.
Manfred Bukofzer, *Music in the Baroque Era.* New York: Norton, 1947.
Hans Gal, ed., *The Musician's World, Great Composers in Their Letters.* New York: Arco, 1966.
Donald J. Grout, *A History of Western Music.* New York: Norton, 1960.
Peter Hansen, *An Introduction to Twentieth Century Music.* Boston: Allyn and Bacon, 1961.
Paul H. Lang, *Music in Western Civilization.* New York: Norton, 1941.
Hugo Leichentritt, *Music, History and Ideas.* Cambridge, Mass.: Harvard University Press, 1938.
Joel Newman, *Renaissance Music.* Englewood Cliffs, N.J.: Prentice-Hall, 1967.
Reinhard G. Pauly, *Music in the Classic Period.* Englewood Cliffs, N.J.: Prentice-Hall, 1965.
Marc Pincherle, *An Illustrated History of Music.* London: Macmillan, 1962.
Eric Salzman, *Twentieth-Century Music: An Introduction.* Englewood Cliffs, N.J.: Prentice-Hall, 1967.
Albert Seay, *Music in the Medieval World.* Englewood Cliffs, N.J.: Prentice-Hall, 1965.
Homer Ulrich and Paul Pisk, *A History of Music and Musical Style.* New York: Harcourt, Brace and World, 1963.
Harold Watkin, *History of Music.* An outline. New York: Monarch, 1962.

### BIOGRAPHIES

An excellent biographical listing is given in the Appendix of William Newman's, *Understanding Music, pp. 301-307.*

# THEORY

### Acoustics
Wilmer Bartholomew, *Acoustics of Music.* Englewood Cliffs, N.J.: Prentice-Hall, 1942.
Leo L. Beranek, *Music, Acoustics and Architecture.* New York: John Wiley, 1962.
Wallace C. Sabine, *Collected Papers on Acoustics.* New York: Dover, 1964.

### Counterpoint
Leslie Bassett, *Manual of 16th Century Counterpoint.* New York: Appleton-Century-Crofts, 1966.
Knud Jeppesen, *Counterpoint.* Translated by Glen Haydon. Englewood Cliffs, N.J.: Prentice-Hall, 1939. Reprinted, 1960.
Walter Piston, *Counterpoint, 18th and 19th Century Styles.* New York: Norton, 1947.
Humphrey Searle, *Twentieth Century Counterpoint.* London: Ernest Benn Limited, 1954.

### Ear Training
Robert Ottman, *Music for Sight Singing.* Englewood Cliffs, N.J.: Prentice-Hall, 1956.

### Form
Paul Fontaine, *Basic Formal Structures in Music.* New York: Appleton-Century-Crofts, 1967.

### Harmony
Christ, DeLone, Kliewer, Rowell, Thomson, *Materials and Structure of Music.* Englewood Cliffs, N.J.: Prentice-Hall, 1966.
Allen I. McHose, *Basic Principles of the Technique of 18th and 19th Century Composition.* New York: Appleton-Century-Crofts, 1951.
Robert Ottman, *Elementary Harmony.* Englewood Cliffs, N.J.: Prentice-Hall, 1961.
Walter Piston, *Harmony.* 3rd ed. New York: Norton, 1962.
Raymond C. Robinson, *Progressive Harmony.* Revised ed. Boston: Bruce Humphries, 1962.

### Orchestration
Kent Kennan, *The Technique of Orchestration.* Englewood Cliffs, N.J.: Prentice-Hall, 1952.
Walter Piston, *Orchestration.* New York: Norton, 1955.

# SPECIAL BOOKS

### American Music
Gilbert Chase, *America's Music.* New York: McGraw-Hill, 1955.
Paul H. Lang, *One Hundred Years of Music in America.* New York: G. Schirmer, 1961.

### Chamber Music
Donald Ferguson, *Image and Structure in Chamber Music.* Minneapolis: University of Minnesota Press, 1964.
Homer Ulrich, *Chamber Music.* 2nd. ed. New York: Columbia University Press, 1966.

### Concerto
Abraham Veinus, *The Concerto.* Rev. republication. New York: Dover, 1964.

### Conducting
Elizabeth Green, *The Modern Conductor.* Englewood Cliffs, N.J.: Prentice-Hall, 1961.
Benjamin Grosbayne, *Techniques of Modern Orchestral Conducting.* Cambridge, Mass.: Harvard University Press, 1956.
Max Rudolf, *The Grammar of Conducting.* New York: G. Schirmer, 1950.

### Musicology
Glen Haydon, *Introduction to Musicology.* Englewood Cliffs, N.J.: Prentice-Hall, 1941. Unaltered reprint. Chapel Hill, N.C.: University of North Carolina Press, 1959.

### Notation
George Heussenstamm, *The Norton Manual of Music Notation.* New York: W. W. Norton, 1987.
Gardner Read, *Music Notation.* New York: Taplinger Publishing Co., 1979.

### Opera
Gladys Davidson, *The Barns Book of the Opera.* New York: Barnes, 1962.
Donald Grout, *A Short History of Opera.* 2 vols. 2nd ed. New York: Columbia University Press, 1965.
Charles Hamm, *Opera.* Boston: Allyn and Bacon, 1966.
Gerhart Westerman, *Opera Guide.* Translated by Anne Rou. New York: E. P. Dutton, 1965.

### Orchestration
Adam Carse, *The History of Orchestration.* New York: Dover, 1964.

### Organ
William Leslie Summer, *The Organ.* 3rd ed. London: MacDonald, 1962.

### Performance
Frederick Dorian, *The History of Music in Performance.* New York: Norton, 1942.

### Solo Song
Denis Stevens, ed. A *History of Song.* London: Hutchinson, 1960.

# APPENDIX E

## GLOSSARY

**A 440 (acoustics)** — A above middle C, equal to 440 vibrations per second. An accepted and adopted standard pitch.
**Absolute music** — Music composed for its own sake, devoid of extra-musical implications.
**Absolute pitch** — The ability to correctly identify sounds heard.
**Acoustics** — The science of sound.
**Anacrusis** *(Gr.)* — Synonomous with up-beat. indicating a melody beginning before the first complete measure.
**Antiphonal** — Opposing bodies of sound, such as one choir answered by another.
**Arrangement** — The adaptation of a composition for an instrument or instruments other than those specified in its original form.
**Atonality** — The absence of key feeling.
**Augmentation** — The lengthening of note values.
**Bitonality** — The use of two different keys simultaneously.
**Cacophony** — Harsh or discordant sounds.
**Cadenza** *(It.)* — An extended solo passage to display the performer's technical skill; usually appears in a concerto before the conclusion of the first movement.
**Chamber music** — Music for a small group of soloists, intended for intimate performance in a small room rather than a large auditorium.
**Chord** — A simultaneous sounding of three or more tones.
**Chromatic** — Tones foreign to a key. A scale comprised of semitones.
**Concerto** — A composition for one or more solo instruments with orchestra.
**Consonance** — A state of relative rest between tones that produces an agreeable effect.
**Contrapuntal** — In the style of counterpoint. Two or more individual melodic parts combined at the same time.
**Counterpoint** — "Note against note." The art of writing independent melodies against each other.
**Development** — The evolution or elaboration of a melody or motive.
**Development section** — The middle portion in a sonata-allegro movement, where the themes and motives are elaborated upon.
**Diatonic** — The natural succession of tones within a scale, excluding chromatic alterations.
**Diminution** — The shortening of note values.
**Dissonance** — A combination of tones that produces unrest and generally creates a disagreeable effect.
**Dodecaphonic music** — Music composed in a twelve-tone series; used synonomously with *twelve-tone music* and *serial music*.
**Embellishment** — Melodic ornamentation consisting of trills, grace notes, runs, etc.
**Enharmonic** — The same pitch given to two different letter names.
**Ensemble** — Any combination or group of singers and/or instrumentalists.
**Episode** — A digression from the main thematic material (in fugal form). A transitory passage (in sonata-allegro form).
**Equal temperament (acoustics)** — A system of tuning whereby the octave is divided into twelve equal semitones.
**Euphony** — Harmonic, pleasant sounding.
**Exposition** — The initial section of a musical form in which the basic thematic material is presented. The first portion of a sonata-allegro movement (exposition, development, recapitulation).
**Form** — The structure of a musical composition.
**Figured bass** — A system of musical shorthand whereby chords are indicated by figures placed below the bass line.
**Fugue** — A highly sophisticated form of imitative counterpoint, comprised of a subject (theme) presented in one voice part and answered (imitated) by another voice or voices in close succession.
**Glissando** *(It.)* — Gliding or sliding; in keyboard music, a scale played by dragging a finger (or fingers) along the keyboard.
**Harmony** — Consonant sounds that produce a pleasing whole. The science of chords and chordal progressions.
**Homophony, Homophonic** — A musical style in which the melody predominates and the accompaniment is subordinate.
**Linear motion** — Scale-wise (step-wise) motion. Horizontal motion.
**Metronome** — A device to indicate the exact tempo of a composition. Invented by John Maelzel in 1815, the metronome indicates any desired number of beats per second.
**Motive** — A brief fragment of a musical theme or subject which may have special melodic and/or rhythmic character.
**Movement** — A main section of a large work such as (first movement) of a sonata, concerto or symphony.
**Musicology** — The scholarly study of music, particularly in the field of history, as differentiated from the art of composition, performance, etc.
**Notation** — The graphic representation of music by symbols that indicate pitch and duration of time.
**Percussive effect** — Strident, sharp, biting sound.
**Phrase** — A natural division of the melodic line, punctuated by some form of cadence (melodic, harmonic, or rhythmic close).
**Polyphony, Polyphonic** — Simultaneous sounding of two or more melodies.
**Polytonal, Polytonality** — The use of several different keys simultaneously.
**Sequence** — The repetition of a melodic pattern at successively higher or lower intervals.
**Sonority** — Richness or fullness of sound.
**Recapitulation** — The reprise or restatement of material already presented. The third portion of the first movement in sonata-allegro form (exposition, development, recapitulation).
**Retrograde** — Moving backwards.
**Rubato** *(It.)* — A free style of playing in which one note may be extended at the expense of another for expressive purposes.
**Serial music** *(See Dodecaphonic music)*.
**Tonality** — The gravitation of a musical composition around a key or tonal center.
**Touch** — The manner in which the keys of the piano are depressed to produce different tone qualities.
**Transcription** *(See Arrangement)*.
**Tune** — A melody or air. The art of adjusting the pitch of an instrument.
**Twelve-tone technique** *(See Dodecaphonic music)*.
**Virtuosity** — Brilliant display of technical facility.

## A DICTIONARY OF MUSICAL TERMS

### TEMPO  Indicates rate of speed.

Largo — broadly, very slowly
Lento — slowly
Adagio — slowly, leisurely
Andante — a walking pace, flowing
Andantino — slightly faster than andante
Moderato — moderately
Allegretto — quickly, but not as fast as allegro
Allegro — at a quick pace, lively
Vivace or Vivo — lively
Presto — very fast
Prestissimo — faster than presto

#### Changing Tempos

Accelerando *(accel.)* to become faster
A tempo — resume original tempo
Mosso — motion
Moto — motion; *(con moto)* with motion,
  or quicker
Rallentando *(rall.)* gradually slowing in speed
Ritardando *(rit.)* becoming slower
Ritenuto *(riten.)* immediate slowing

### DYNAMICS  Pertaining to the volume of sound.

Pianissimo *(pp)* very soft
Piano *(p)* soft
Mezzo piano *(mp)* moderately soft
Mezzo forte *(mf)* moderately loud
Forte *(f)* loud
Fortissimo *(ff)* very loud
Sforzando *(sfz )* strong accent

#### Changing Dynamics

Crescendo *(cresc.)* growing louder
Decrescendo *(decresc.)* growing softer
Diminuendo *(dim., dimin.)* growing softer

### STYLE  The character or mood of the composition.

Animato — animated, with spirit
Brio — vigor, spirit
Cantabile — singing
Dolce — sweetly
Espressivo *(espress.)* with expression, feeling
Giocoso — humorously
Grazioso — gracefully
Legato *(leg.)* smoothly connected tones
Maestoso — majestically
Marcia — as a march
Portamento — slightly disconnected tones
Scherzando — playfully
Sostenuto — sustained
Staccato *(stacc.)* disconnected tones
Tenuto *(ten.)* held note
Tranquillo — calm, quiet, tranquil

### MISCELLANEOUS TERMS

Coda — ending
Con — with
D. C. *(Da Capo)* go to the beginning
D. C. al Fine — repeat from the beginning
                to the end (Fine)
D. S. *(Dal Segno)* the sign 𝄋
D. S. al Fine — repeat from the sign to the end (Fine)
Fermata — pause, or hold the note 𝄐
Fine — the end
Loco — in normal location or pitch register
Meno — less
Molto — much
Non — not
Piu — more
Poco — a little
Poco a poco — little by little, gradually
Sempre — always
Simile — in a similar way
Troppo — too much

### NOTES AND RESTS

𝅝  whole note          𝄻  whole rest
𝅗𝅥  half note           𝄼  half rest
𝅘𝅥  quarter note        𝄽  quarter rest
𝅘𝅥𝅮  eighth note         𝄾  eighth rest
𝅘𝅥𝅯  sixteenth note      𝄿  sixteenth rest
𝅘𝅥𝅰  thirty-second note  𝅀  thirty-second rest

𝅘𝅥𝅮  grace note — to be played quickly

𝄇  arpeggiated, or rolled chord

### SIGNS

♯ — sharp
♭ — flat
♮ — natural
𝄐 — fermata
. — staccato

𝄪 — double sharp
♭♭ — double flat
*8va* — octave

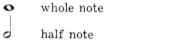 — portamento

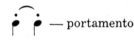 — triplet

⌐1. ⌐2. ⌐ — first and second endings

‾ > ^ — stress, accent, strong accent

**C** *(common time)* 4 beats to the measure *(4/4)*
**¢** *(alla breve)* 2 strong beats to the measure *(2/2)*

𝄇 repeat sign

tied notes

slurred notes

Ped., P, └──┘   ∧──∧ — pedal indications